TRUE
NORTH

TRUE NORTH

*a collection of stories
to guide you home*

TINA ADDORISIO • ASHLEY ANTONIETTA
JOVANA BOROJEVIC • DANA CLARK • SHANNON HARLOW
MARGARITA KALIKA • ASHLEY-ANN PEREIRA
DANIELLE ROSA • DEVLYN SARAH • MELISSA SEGUIN

TRUE NORTH
A Collection of Stories to Guide You Home

© 2020 Collective Voices

COVER & TEXT DESIGN BY Jazmin Welch
COVER PHOTO BY Kyle Cottrell on Unsplash
EDITED BY The Studio Press
PUBLISHED BY The Studio Press

ISBN 978-1-7771734-0-1

To you,
May this book shine light on your True North.

contents

message to the reader

To you, the reader,
We see you.

We know that you have a story that has shaped you into who you are today, just as our stories have molded us and guided us back home, to our true selves, to our true north.

As a collective, we said yes to sharing our voices in hopes to help guide you back home to your own true north.

So, as you dive into our stories, we want to ask you, what's your message?

With Love,
The Collective Voices

The Wild
Way Home

MARGARITA KALIKA

"Just when the caterpillar thought her world was over,
she became a butterfly."
Ancient Proverb (edited pronouns)

AUTHOR'S NOTE: I will be addressing my body as "her" rather than "it" to bridge from seeing "her" as an object to a living expression.

LOST IN DARKNESS

"Yes, but you will always be looking for the essence," she drawled.

I sat there in a tiny room at a basic round table. Nothing flashy. No crystal balls or velvety royal purple chairs. In this most plain room, the psychic dished out the answer to my "Will I get married?" question.

Up until then I had no idea what "essence" meant except that I had always been a sensitive child writing poetry and watching the stars. When I sat with the psychic, I was in my early twenties struggling with a pile of rocks on my heart: an unfulfilling relationship, confusion with my life path while studying Politics, and, most painfully, an eating disorder.

As a child, I remember having a light spirit. I chased butterflies and laid belly-down on the grass watching grasshoppers hop. This feeling of freedom to be my sunshine self ended abruptly at eight-years-old. During a family outing, I was admiring my reflection in a compact mirror by the water. I remember feeling like a mermaid on a rock. Later in the day, a family acquaintance at the time whispered to me in quick Russian that I would *always be the fat girl*. Instantly my face burned. My heart sank like an anchor and hid in the darkness of shame and self-hatred. It no longer felt safe to just be me.

For almost two decades, I detested mirrors and avoided the water whenever I could. I never wanted to see or show myself again.

Eventually, at twenty-years-old, this self-hatred and avoidance of my pain took the twisted shape of anorexia. It began innocently with trying to manage my diet with healthier options. Then quickly, it led to an uncontrollable downward spiral where managing my diet morphed into severe food restriction and obsession. Anorexia feels like having a dictator enter your mind, take a seat on a throne, and incessantly command what you do every single minute of your day. I began food restricting and ignoring my body's desperation to be fed. I believed that by emptying myself, there would be nothing left to see and then I would be protected from ever being attacked for my body again. I would be accepted for being nothing and it would be *that* that would make me matter in the world.

The irony about possessing a disordered body image is that while I intensely focused on my body, I was so far outside of her. I was clinging and searching for something *out there* to save me from feeling unwanted like a fish gasping for air. My energy fed obsessive thoughts of, *Who is watching me and what do they think about what they see?*

Anorexia had me carefully sculpt every area of myself and my life to perfection. I kept a busy routine with a relationship with my then long-term boyfriend, maintaining honours in university, excessively exercising, and working as a Supervisor. From the outside, I looked like I was shining, but on the inside I was completely dull. It was not until the nighttime that I could hear my body in pain trying to get my attention. She could not sleep with stomach pains and begged me for something, *anything*. I still did not listen, I carried on. I was too afraid to give her what she was asking for because I believed that what she wanted would lead me to rejection and unworthy to be seen. In fact, I punished her for being called fat and I blamed my inner child for being the wrong shape. As my anorexia intensified, so did the pain. Everyday I had near fainting spells in washrooms and intense body aches. I never had a break from the voice that would hammer in my mind about how worthless I was no matter how hard I tried to satisfy requests to starve and deny my body. I was a prisoner like a butterfly trapped in her cocoon.

On my 22nd birthday, my sister gifted me a necklace with the words etched, *"Just when the caterpillar thought her world was over, she became a butterfly."* Little did she know how intensely I was suffering inside by that time. As simple as the gesture was, I was holding a treasure. Each word was like a piece of a mosaic and together I felt their light beaming through into my heart like sunlight illuminating stained glass. I could feel myself grasp just a little tighter on the edge of the cliff I was barely holding onto. Inside I heard a small whisper, "Hold on a little longer." Emanating from this small piece of silver was enough light to give me hope of freedom for the first time in years.

Eventually, at twenty-five years old, the life I created to shield pain and escape from myself crumbled. No longer did I have romantic partnerships or other external validations to escape to. For the first time in my life, while living alone in my own apartment, I found myself facing my own darkness. I was finally going in.

STUMBLING UPON LIGHT

I believe that one of the ways that Spirit speaks to us is in signs and symbols. For me living alone in a big city, they came in the form of heart shapes everywhere I went. On a sunny Autumn day, I left my new apartment for a walk. As I passed by a children's school, I noticed painted on a large poster were the different life stages of a butterfly. Observing each phase, I quietly whispered to Spirit, "How can I go from pushing through the cocoon to finally bursting out as a butterfly?" Immediately I felt an inner nudge to look directly down at my feet. There laid a small pink heart made of glitter foam. Then I spotted more of these hearts all around me like sweetly scattered rose petals. Love. *Of course.* It was the energy that would carry me through healing and was the eventual answer I would discover to, *What am I really made of beyond the pounds and measurements.*

As more time in solitude passed, I slowly reconnected with my heart and body. It was like climbing down into the shadows to free my eight-year-old self. A swirl of energy released within me. My body's desperation to eat became louder and I finally heeded her call one spoonful at a time. This came at a heavy price as my ego wanted to cling onto its lifeboat of perfection. Very carefully and painfully, I began eating again. At first, my body reached for anything I offered her, begging for more quantity. I fed her while horrified to eat properly again so for some time I held onto a dizzying pendulum swing of extreme food restriction and overeating. My body was a wreck. While I felt like I was losing control, the truth is anorexia had already been drowning me to please others and dismiss myself. It had locked me into its controlling grip all along. As I stared at each meal that I had prepared for myself, I discovered that I was not in fact giving in, but rather surrendering to love.

Healing is not a straight path from pain to bliss. My road zig-zagged sometimes off the edge where my thoughts would push me back into a cage again to stop eating. Eventually amidst this chaos, a gentle yet fierce voice within me surfaced. She repeated, "Just trust, this is all a part of the healing. You are healing." I recognized her as my highest self of all, my soul. Even when I relapsed, I now had a fighting spirit questioning the anorexic thoughts and bringing me back to the table over and again.

As I was tending to my immediate physical survival, I knew that I would have to shift from simply focusing on my plate to staring at myself again. All the years of self-hatred had me looking through distorted lenses that made it impossible to see my beauty. Now I needed to truly look at myself again so that I could develop clear vision. I practiced self gazing where I stared at myself in a mirror. It was not with the same mermaid-like wild abandon I had at eight-years-old. This time, I saw eyes that had been tightly kept shut to her suffering and now needed to release. Through tears, I adamantly met my gaze even with a resistant mind. The more I looked *into* myself, I felt the mask of perfectionism dissolve. While I was terrified to let go of the mask, I knew it was not me and I had to be okay with this. I dove deeper.

I saw that anorexia was a tightly knotted ball of thoughts in my mind around unworthiness and unbelonging. Every thought was a possession, like objects cluttering my inner home. It was my choice to select what I held inside. Every time I looked in the mirror, I saw eyes tired of the battle. For many years after my experience at eight-years-old, I obsessively turned over in my mind what the man said to me: *Was it true that nothing else would ever matter about me if I were "the fat girl"?* But this time while staring into the mirror, I began asking soulful questions: "Does how someone sees me make me less worthy? What do *I* see myself made of?" It was not overnight, but eventually I saw rainbow light peeking through my eyes again. I had reclaimed my place on the rock. I was coming home.

FINDING HOME

When I stopped chasing the thing that always escaped me— love from "somewhere else"—I remapped to come back home to myself. I believe that each of us answer a call to walk our self-love journey however painful. The journey submerges you into darkness to discover the nature of your light. Of all the places you have been, it is back to yourself you come home to.

I do still stray from the path home to myself, but I have learned this is a natural spiral of healing. Gently bring yourself back. For a long time, I resisted putting my hand on my heart or touching my stomach. I cried during many yoga practices because I had to literally be in touch with myself and I could not bear that level of intimacy and vulnerability. I resisted taking deep breaths because that would mean I would have to feel my body physically expanding. While I detested the feeling of expansion, eventually it felt more painful to live in a constant state of contraction. Coming back into your own body in this way feels different than judging and shaming her. You allow her to breathe again like having another chance at life.

Allow me to remind you—the precious reader of my story—that you belong. Your vibrant presence is needed here. Giving someone else the measuring stick to determine whether you fit into this world or not is like drinking poison. It is emptying to whittle your life, measuring yourself against others and fitting into tight boxes that your heart is too bright for, bursting to break free. Seek a treasured life of going in to discover your riches—your true worth. Nothing else may feel as important as being accepted, but your belonging is not beholden to others making room for you based on their requirements. Your place is amongst the beauty of Earth that sustains all life, gifting you wild lands to explore yourself. As you choose to heal, remember that you must live in the darkness of soil to burst through and bloom. Reach deeper into yourself to come up higher as your true self.

Your inner landscape is deeply layered and textured. When you are diving in, it is natural to face murky waters. You are navigating and moving through years or perhaps decades of built-up-internalized toxic ideas and beliefs that you have been mostly unconsciously living in. Keep moving through the mess as you meet what you wish to belong to you and what to dissolve. It is tempting to hide amongst the pressures and expectations of others rather than leading with a courageous heart to meet *your* truth. Let the waters clear. To remain silent and hidden in lies and illusions keeps you entangled on the superficial surface, blocking the deeper current connecting you to your soul. Reclaim your power and release your butterfly spirit made for transformation and renewal.

As you begin to listen to the wisdom of your soul, teach your mind each day to speak kindly to yourself. Learn how to open your heart again. And, most importantly, promise your body that she is in your loving and trusting hands again. Spend your whole life tending to this sacred relationship. Healing anorexia illuminated that I deserve the freedom of love, peace, and joy because that is the light I am made of. You do not have to try to win it from the outside. Choose to end the battle. When you put down the sword, you surrender the fight with yourself and with the negative energies of your past and present. True freedom is breathing in your own light again to shine out.

No matter what your self-love struggles have morphed into, remember that you are the keeper of wisdom about yourself. You are not a lump of clay to be sculpted to distorted perfection, but rather a treasure to be experienced and held. Anorexia taught me the painful truth that I cannot leave the matters of my heart—my worth, soul purpose, and reason for being—to another to shape me. Discover what moves you and makes you come alive so that you may lead an enriching life authored by your own hand.

As I close the chapter to this part of my healing path, may it open the door to yours. The search for the elusive essence is over. No matter where you are, trust that you are moving towards your essence of light and love. It lies inside each of us buried in our wild and untamed nature. Welcome yourself back home under sunlight with a mirror in hand seeing yourself clearly and shining bright. Plunge back into the magical waters to continue the discovery of the ever-unfolding beauty that is you.

Birthing
From Within

MELISSA SEGUIN

"In giving birth to our babies, we may find that we birth new possibilities within ourselves."

Jon Kabat-Zinn

TUNING IN

I closed the door and walked into the cool night air, feeling both completely calm and totally confused. *What did it all mean?*, I wondered. Time would soon tell.

It was my first experience with Reiki, a Japanese healing modality that helps the body tap into its own innate ability to heal on all levels. I had been intrigued for a while and after hearing about a friend's experience with this practitioner, I booked an appointment on a whim.

After that initial appointment, it was business as usual, but I continued to think about my session and wondered what would come of it. Then, I got my period, and mine and my husband's life changed forever.

I got into the car and he asked, "How was your day?"

I looked at him with tears in my eyes and said, "I got my period today."

He looked at me confused, "Isn't that a good thing?"

"I guess so, but I feel disappointed and truly sad and I'm not sure why," I said.

"Did you think you were pregnant? It's not as though we were trying," he voiced.

"I know," I said, "but I just can't shake how I feel."

Then I remembered my appointment from a few days earlier and it all started to make sense. The tears came again. I vividly remembered the baby that came so clearly to me in a vision while receiving the Reiki. That gorgeous child with huge brown eyes must have been for me. *Could it be? Am I supposed to be a mom?* My faith allowed me to trust that it was a sign and it was for me to contemplate. It felt strange, scary, surreal and exciting all at the same time. I needed to make sense of it.

Unlike some of my friends who dreamed of becoming mothers since the day they were born, it wasn't a desire of mine. In fact, I was adamant that I did not want children and I had my parents convinced that I wouldn't be making them grandparents; they were obviously disappointed.

When I met my husband, he was neither here nor there about children. Much like any serious couple, we had many discussions about our future and whether or not we would choose to welcome children into our life. We decided that if it happened we would welcome a child, but we would not actively plan for one.

We had an amazing life. We both worked at great jobs. We lived in a condo downtown and loved living in the city. We came and went as we pleased. We travelled when we wanted to, wherever we wanted to. We dined out at a moment's notice. We enjoyed the bar and club scene while also continuing our studies.

It wasn't an ideal time to start a family. I was in my second year of homeopathic medicine, while working full time as a massage therapist. My husband was set to write his second of three CFA exams, while also working in the corporate world. But, I couldn't shake the feeling inside. The desire was there, I think. The seed had been planted and I couldn't stop thinking about it all. I literally became obsessed with wanting a baby, stat.

It took some convincing, but my husband finally agreed with the idea of having a child. We began trying immediately for that big eyed baby I had visions of in that Reiki session. Knowing that it could take time, but praying it didn't, I tuned into the trust I felt within. That baby was for us, I was sure of it. Sure enough, it happened very quickly and to this day we feel very blessed, as we know that's not always the case.

It was just before 6:00 am on the day after my period was due, I was about to pee on a stick to see whether or not we were pregnant. I was shaking, but not in the way I had been when I had done a pregnancy test in the past. This time, instead of praying for a negative result, I was worried that it would indeed be negative and I would be terribly disappointed. Those were the longest seconds of my life. I wasn't the type to pee and then not stare at the stick. You better believe I watched those lines fill in, revealing that I was indeed going to be a mama. I stared at the stick and started to shake, "holy shit" I said, "this is real life right now." I walked into the bedroom and said "congrats babe—we're over achievers."

"What are you talking about?" he asked, still half asleep. I showed him the test and told him he was going to be a papa. He didn't believe me. I mean it could have been that it was before 6:00 am on a Saturday morning or maybe he was disappointed that the process didn't take more time, *if you know what I mean.* Regardless we were both feeling a little of everything. *Did we really think this through? Is this really happening? How are we so fortunate? Are we really going to become parents?*

Now what?

TRUSTING

The next few weeks were a blur. It was Chinese take-out daily because that's all I could stomach. 7:00 pm bedtimes and lots of discussion about how the next steps would go. We decided to have our baby under the care of a midwife and we were lucky to get in with a midwife we adored and trusted. We also decided to hire a doula who was also a homeopathic doctor. Homeopathic medicine at that time had been my primary form of medicine for years and I trusted it. You see, we had a plan for our birth and we wanted it to be as natural as possible. We decided, through careful consideration, to birth our baby at home. The months passed uneventfully. We had decided not to find out the sex of our baby because well, life is too predictable most of the time and we delighted in the uncertainty. We welcomed the surprise.

On August 6th at about 11:00 pm I began having, what felt like, could be contractions. I thought, *oh my gosh, this is it, we're about to meet our baby*. Throughout the night the contractions advanced. We decided a walk to the market that morning might help bring us closer to meeting our baby. Having to stop for some very strong contractions made for a long and tedious walk. After arriving home we called our doula to let her know that labour had started. She asked if we needed her, but I told her I'd be fine for a while longer. I decided to get in the shower to ease some of the discomfort and it worked so well that my contractions started to get easier and further apart. At that point my intuition told me that I needed to get out of the shower, despite the fact that my physical body was so happy for the relief. Slowly the contractions started to pick up again and finally, late afternoon, our doula came over. We also called our midwife to check in with her and she decided to come check on us and arrived at about 6:00 pm. With each contraction, now about 4 to 5 minutes apart, she could tell I was in a lot of pain. Upon checking I was only 2–3 cm dilated. I was so disheartened and frustrated. I felt I had been working so hard all day and that we were surely getting closer. At this point she told me her suspicions that my baby might be an occiput posterior, also known as, sunny side up or, the opposite of how a baby should ideally be positioned for delivery. This would explain the tremendous back and hip pain I was experiencing with each contraction. As the labour continued we discussed with our midwife the idea of rupturing my water. Despite having planned for minimal medical intervention, the reality was that I had been in labour for about 20 hours and I was still only 3 cm dilated. We heavily weighed the pros and cons and decided to go ahead with the procedure, it felt like the right choice. Looking back, I am so thankful I trusted this decision. Upon breaking my water, we discovered that my water contained meconium, which meant an automatic transfer to hospital. We moved quickly and I tearfully said goodbye to the homebirth experience that I had envisioned.

Thankfully, despite being at the hospital, I was still under the care of my midwife, but now I was also being monitored by doctors and nurses. It was a bit of a surreal experience as they were robotic and business as usual. My progress, regardless of my ruptured water, was not really moving and the contractions were getting stronger and harder each time. Homeopathy helped to take the edge off, but the truth was that I was exhausted. I began to question my body and whether it could really do what it was meant to do. The thoughts in my mind became erratic and delusional. As time passed and the contractions grew stronger and longer I wondered how I would be strong enough to birth our baby. I think the exhaustion coupled with the lack of control really played with my mind. Not to mention, our birth plan had literally been thrown out the window.

After a quick check, my midwife reported that I was 4–5 cm dilated. This felt like progress, but it wasn't happening fast enough. At that point she suggested an epidural. *An epidural?* I couldn't believe I was hearing this from her and she could see my questioning. She also knew that the most important aspect of my birth plan was a vaginal birth. She told me that I needed to rest so that I would have the energy when the time came to push my baby out. I hesitantly agreed.

After the epidural, I was checked by the doctor on call. It was around midnight and she warned that if I wasn't ready to push by 6:00 am that she would be doing a c-section.

As the night slowly passed, I worked with my mind to help my baby come naturally. I felt like maybe I could will my body into dilation and I could avoid the confrontation with the doctor about how I would not be going for a c-section and instead would continue to trust my body and my baby. But, there was that underlying concern they talked about, the meconium. Meconium can be very dangerous, I understood that, but my baby was not showing any signs of distress so this was my upper hand and I would use it to advocate for my desired vaginal birth.

Thankfully, by 6:00 am I was fully dilated and it was time to push, avoiding the c-section that I desperately didn't want. Later, we were gifted a team of doctors that were relatable and with whom I felt comfortable with to catch our baby.

Pushing to bring my baby into the world was by far some of the hardest and most powerful work I have ever done. I'm not gonna lie, I had to dig deep, trust and find my bravery, all the while believing my body was capable. But it was one hurdle after another and I was exhausted. I had been in labour for more than thirty hours. I was battling anger and sadness. I felt that the epidural took away the connection I felt earlier with my baby, that I so desperately needed to feel now. I could no longer feel anything and I knew deep down that this wasn't how it should go. For 40 weeks we had had a partnership and in the last hours before my baby was born I felt as though I failed on my end of that partnership. People will always tell you, you do what you have to do to have a healthy baby and while I did believe that, it didn't change the overwhelming sadness I was feeling inside, like I had already failed our relationship in some way.

Finally, at 9:02 am on August 8th, our baby boy was born. Because of the meconium, he was quickly taken away for examination but thankfully, he was perfectly healthy and he was already showing us how strong his lungs were. I was immediately overwhelmed with all the feelings. He was safe and healthy and I was thankful. I was relieved that it was finally over and astonished at what I had just accomplished on very little to no sleep and zero food. I was impressed with how hungry I felt and regretful that things didn't go as planned. I was shocked that I was now a mama and that my baby boy indeed had the biggest eyes I had ever seen.

The next few days, weeks, and months were a blurry haze. I was the most exhausted I have ever felt, but at the same time I was experiencing what true unconditional love meant. The dichotomy was striking in those early days. I struggled a lot of the days, but as I learned to trust myself and follow that deep down 'mama-feeling,' we began to find our rhythm. Those initial months were some of the hardest months of my life. I had to adjust to life as it would now be, come to terms with losing my own freedom and life as I knew it. Adjusting to a whole new identity and feeling like I didn't get a chance to say goodbye to the old one. But underneath all of these emotions I still couldn't release the feeling that I started this mama journey already failing my sweet baby boy. This would take time and trust in order to heal. Each day I found myself searching for ways to feel that connection with my boy. Each day I would pray he felt my efforts. I knew I had to trust that how he came into this world and how I mothered him was enough. It still sat with me and would eventually take some therapy to finally forgive myself.

GIFTS

Through all of this, I learned that we must always trust ourselves. We must question things we are presented with and tune into ourselves and to what our intuition is telling us. Exploring that deep down feeling of knowing and questioning, we must ask ourselves the hard questions and pay attention to the answers that come; trusting in our physical bodies and learning to advocate for ourselves. At the very least, have someone in our corner that knows how to do it when we are not quite capable. We have to recognize that something bigger than ourselves is always at play, call it god, spirit, or source. We are never in control and so we must trust that all is how it is meant to be.

In case you're wondering, I did get another chance at that homebirth. It was a beautiful, uneventful homebirth, as we welcomed another baby boy two years later. The gift of my first birth was that I learned to let go of control. I learned to trust myself on a deeper level. I trusted my body and my mind. I learned that my body could birth a baby vaginally, something I trusted but didn't know for sure the first time around. I learned that despite what happens, I will always have a deep connection to my babies simply because I am their mama. It was these gifts of my first birth that allowed me to easily trust that I could work with my baby and together we could have the homebirth we were meant to experience.

Giving birth is a beautiful, raw, powerful and surreal experience. It's like nothing else and quite honestly the two most vivid memories I have. The details I still remember almost eight and ten years later quite literally blow my mind. I sometimes wish I wanted more children simply to be able to experience the immense emotions that come with giving birth. When we add that spiritual layer to it we are able to deeply feel the emergence of life, literally from within. I wouldn't change either of my birth stories. Just thinking of them empowers me to this day. The gifts that each of them have taught me are like none I have learned. Trust, empowerment, hope, belief and how to let go fully and embrace each second, each moment for what they are. These births taught me my super powers and for both experiences I will forever be grateful.

My wish is that you find empowerment through my story. That you dig deep on trusting yourself. That you recognize your strength and super powers through your own stories of grit, resilience, belief and trust. May we all be blessed to know ourselves deeper.

Love Starts From Within, All Else Follows

ASHLEY ANTONIETTA

Who are you?

I remembered asking myself this, barely breathing. I had just finished having my second anxiety attack that day. I looked at myself in the mirror and didn't recognize the girl looking back at me. I felt completely powerless.

Why did I stay for so long?

I believed I was worthless and undeserving of love, but as time passed, I began realizing that it had nothing to do with him. His verbal abuse and manipulation triggered these feelings, as these types of characteristics in a man had triggered me before, enforcing the beliefs I had created.

Who had I become to allow it?

This was the real question that helped me start to uncover patterns and behaviors within myself that attracted such relationships.

I was twenty-eight years old at the time. I wanted to create a life of love by getting married and having children so badly. This was my dream and it became my sole focus to the point that I allowed myself to *almost* achieve this goal no matter the repercussions. Even if it meant I had to sacrifice my own happiness. I had completely lost my power during those four years of what seemed to be the longest relationship of my life.

We lived together in the dream home we created that was symbolic of the future ahead of us. I had worked so hard to get to this place of fulfillment. I would excuse and defend my relationship at all times feeling so far away from myself to save face with my family and friends. *No one would understand,* I thought to myself. This had been the second-long term relationship that would have been a failure; this is how I saw it.

How would I bear another failure?

I believed that honoring myself was wrong and how it looked or felt to others around me was more important. That was my belief. I thought that breaking up with someone after four years, who I had already moved in with, was seen as irresponsible. I wanted my family and friends to approve of my choices and I feared that leaving this established relationship would disappoint them. I was anxious all the time, barely breathing, in my day to day. My anxiety took over and occupied all my time. I did anything and everything to keep busy to avoid having to deal with what I knew to be true inside my heart. I wasn't happy.

One weekend, my parents came over for a surprise visit. As they pulled onto our street, I was pulling out and found myself feeling angry at them for showing up unexpectedly; I wasn't prepared to put on the happy face. I rushed them away and lied about being late to where I was headed. My parents looked at me and said, "Honey, are you okay? Can't you go later? We are here now." I declined and told them I didn't have time and that I had to hurry back to cook dinner.

I occupied my time with many things to do to fulfill my role as the women of the house. The house always had to be in perfect condition. Food was always freshly cooked no matter what time of day or night. That's what he expected, and I willingly fulfilled his needs even if they weren't aligned with my truths.

This wasn't the first relationship I had experienced that was disempowering. Previous to this, I was engaged at twenty-three years old and felt embarrassed to leave.

One day as I was walking down the stairs, on my way out to meet my fiancé, my dad stopped me at the bottom of the stairs. "Honey, why are you in such a rush, breathe. Are you okay?" I tried to go around him to avoid making eye contact and just as I took another step, he held my hand and with tears in his eyes said, "If you want to call off the wedding I will take care of everything. I fully support you." At that moment, I let my dad in. I dropped to my knees while he held me and expressed how embarrassed and ashamed I felt. I told him how scared I was knowing that this wasn't right for me.

I was engaged to an older man who had similar tendencies of being short tempered and overly controlling as the man I was in a relationship with at twenty-eight. I admired this older man as he provided a view of a life that I thought I wanted.

Was I really going to call off my wedding two months before it was supposed to happen? What would my grandparents think of me? I was lucky to have all four grandparents present and their views and perspectives at the time, meant the world to me. I wanted them to be proud of me as they were for my cousins who were married before me. Once again, I had followed the same patterns of silencing my inner guidance out of fear of what others would think of me. The invitations were ready to be sent out, while my wedding dress hung delicately on it's hanger. The venue was paid in full, the details booked, organized and ready to be executed come the big day.

In that moment, at the bottom of the stairs, my dad gave me the greatest gift. He modelled to me what it would look like to honor myself and take my power back regardless of how hard of a decision it may be. He was an example of strength that taught me how to be a strong woman. Somewhere along the way, I lost sight of his teachings.

With his support, the wedding was called off.

As I moved from one relationship to the next, repeating the same patterns and attracting the same types of men, I experienced multiple scary surgeries. My Doctor had discovered I had cancerous cells in my cervix. My body had been responding to all of the discomfort I was feeling in my relationships as I suppressed all of my suffering. I was told that I may not be able to bear a child one day, which broke me even further. I remember my mom being with me at every single appointment and holding my hand as I was told the news. It was yet another indicator for me to begin my awakening journey. My mother was my pillar when I felt my whole world crumbling before me. She was my strength when I felt the weakest.

From then on, I began my journey inward and started asking myself questions that held space for me to shift. I also started to see a therapist. His guidance and support was a gift. He helped me change my entire perspective. It was the greatest investment in myself. I started to realize that the questions I was previously asking myself, weren't helping me align with the outcomes I was yearning for.

He constantly reminded me to not focus on my ex and all he had done to hurt me. He empowered me to ask questions like, "What have you thought of yourself to allow someone to treat you that way? "How much do you value your worth if you continue to be in a relationship that makes you feel unworthy?" In one of our sessions he bravely interjected while I was mid sentence, my eyes full of tears and said, "I don't want to hear about him anymore. I want to understand where you're at to have allowed and attracted this reality." In that moment he gave me a new awareness, a beautiful gift. You see, I was focusing on the wrong emotions. I was focusing on blaming everyone who had wronged me, which took my power away. Although yes, these emotions were valid, and the experiences were real, focusing on them wouldn't allow me to move forward with the new empowered perspective I was beginning to create for myself.

My journey to self-discovery began as I was redefining myself in ways I had never done before. While I discovered a new version of myself, the healing process became intertwined in a powerful and profound way.

So what next?

I began with asking myself different questions that were particularly focused on a) feeling better and b) being in alignment with what I truly wanted. I wanted to love and be loved unconditionally. As I asked different questions, I began gaining clarity.

What I realized was that my relationship with myself was more important than my relationship with anyone else. I desired a relationship with myself that was full of unconditional love and self-care. I now know that the root of all external relationships is dependent on the internal one we have with ourselves and how necessary it is to create this with yourself first. This was one of my profound realizations and it became my new belief.

If I had focused on developing a relationship with my inner self, all relationships I encountered would follow suit. I quickly realized that at that time, I didn't love myself. I had limiting beliefs about not being worthy of love, not being desirable or attractive enough. Because of these beliefs, I would find every opportunity to be with others, so that I wasn't alone; hoping they'd fill the void and lack I felt. I *also* realized that this was the belief that created my anxiety. I was constantly filling this void with other people and keeping so busy that I couldn't even catch my breath.

I lived with anxiety for three years. I didn't openly share this with many. I would have multiple panic attacks per day, while having no control or remedies to deal with them. When I went to see my doctor, she suggested going on medication. At that moment, I knew a shift was needed. I started to find natural ways to deal with anxiety. I found moments to sit in meditation, even though at first it felt impossible to sit with myself at all. I began to educate myself on how to prevent anxiety, with an understanding that it would be challenging to manage because once one has experienced an attack, it becomes more difficult to calm. So I made a commitment to myself to sit in meditation. I found other ways to sit with myself, for example I'd make bracelets that turned into a healing tool for me. Creating and using my hands calmed me. This practice eventually turned into a small business of creating bead bracelets for others with the intention of not focusing on the power of the gemstone, even though they hold power, but instead focusing on the power within ourselves. This continued to heal me. I shared my new insights and lessons with others about the power we have within, that we don't need external people or things to fill ourselves.

As I continued with daily mediation and making bead bracelets, I started to journal. Writing was something I hadn't done for many years. Before I started this new journey, I wrote mainly about negative experiences and thoughts. When I committed to begin writing again, I wrote about everything I was uncovering in my new way of being. I wrote about all I was unlearning, redefining, what I had created and how I was starting to feel much stronger. Tony Robbins inspired me to write about all the things I was grateful for. He had been someone who, in my eyes, had this power to inspire and enlighten several people at one time. I looked up to his strength and his teachings as a way to uncover the power within myself. I started to tap into the teachings of other enlightened teachers such as Esther Hicks. Her softness and beautiful expression about following our inner knowing, was endearing to me. She taught me about focus and how focus creates all things.

I made major changes during this time in my life. I booked a trip to Italy on my own. I had only booked a few locations to visit with family, but most of the trip was left unplanned. I had never gone away on my own before; I typically defaulted to very planned and scheduled trips with others. I hadn't embraced travelling in this new-found way. I was always so calculated in having everything planned out. I lost sight of what it truly felt like to be in the now. That trip truly propelled me into my new way of being. I had discovered this new confidence within myself. I felt like I could do anything. For the first time in a very long time, I felt free and connected to my child-like self. I surprised myself completely. It was the first time I had ever truly enjoyed my own company. While exploring Italy, I didn't feel a sense of lack, instead I felt whole and developed a euphoric high for life. I remember looking at myself in the mirror, while in Santa Margherita, and for the first time, I was able to see a sparkly glow in my eyes. I was home. I had found myself in the woman I was becoming.

Later that year, I celebrated the purchase of my very own condo and I completed everything from the legal meetings and signing of paperwork on my own. I felt liberated. I was free and so much stronger knowing that I had everything I needed within me. That condo sparked a newfound independence as I lived farther from family. It was an opportunity to create something brand new. I moved to the city of Toronto and became a downtown girl, which is something I thought I'd never do. I remember bugging my little sister about how living in the city wasn't sustainable and that she should move closer to the suburbs where our family lived. It was uncomfortable and at times I felt disconnected from all that was familiar, including my family, but it provided me with a peaceful place to heal and feel safe again. I completely transformed my condo, getting into all the interior design details. I took the opportunity to really create a place from within. I began to understand what it felt like to live in a mindfully created space from how I wanted to feel.

Just like that, I was given another gift. I discovered my true passion for design and as I connected the dots I uncovered what it felt like to create a life through manifestation and focus. I was laser focused on feeling good, while being conscious of my choices and what I surrounded myself with. A couple of years later, I met the absolute love of my life; the man who changed it all. He has added so much magic to my life. As I entered this new relationship, I felt so different because I was already whole by myself. I overflowed with so much love and gratitude with an understanding that he would become an extension of that in my life. We had known of each other from high school, but we never really spoke. He wasn't someone I would've typically dated, but I knew in that moment after our first date that I had manifested it all. I didn't doubt or question anything that was unfolding. I had this inner knowing and trust that he appeared when and how he was meant to. Fast forward two and a half years later and we now live in an area of the city that we absolutely adore. It's an area that I had my eye on when I made my first condo purchase. Together, we've bought our dream home where we can raise our family.

As I continued to heal and create more love and joy in my life, I started to focus less on all the lack I once felt. I even began to believe that one day I would get pregnant and I would know in that moment that everything was perfect as it is. As I write this, I am three months pregnant with our first child. When I found out I was pregnant, it felt like an out of body experience. I was so happy and the most interesting part is that I wasn't surprised because I knew in my heart that through my healing and rediscovery, I would create all that I desired.

And so it is.

Awakening to Embrace Imperfection

SHANNON HARLOW

> *"Surrender to what is. Let go of what was.*
> *Have faith in what will be."*
> **Sonia Ricotti**

As I slowly open my eyes, adjusting to the harsh hospital lights, a wave of confusion washes over me. *Where am I?*

Last I recall I was driving home from grocery shopping with my daughter, Sydney. We were in the car, belting out the lyrics to 'Lucid Dreams' by Juice World, anticipating our wakeup by the lake the following morning. Then, I'm told there had been a car crash. This isn't the cottage haven where I was intending to wake up. Instead, I'm in a hospital bed unable to move and speak with a breathing and feeding tube in my throat. Tubes were coming from everywhere. A brace was holding my neck in place and I was unable to ask my family, *what is happening?*

There I was unable to walk, speak, eat or drink. I'm confused and scared, and I'm in the most unlikely place... a hospital.

Later, I learned that a police officer showed up at our house. When my husband, Bill, answered the door he was given the terrible news that Sydney and I had been in an accident just down the road. The police officer told him that my daughter and I were taken to different hospitals and Bill responded with, "Oh my God!" and as a wave of fear washed over him he expressed, "What an impossible decision, where do I go? Do I go to my daughter or to my wife?" The police officer said, "Well in my opinion, you need to go to your wife. Your daughter is injured, but it is not life threatening. Your wife's injuries are indeed life threatening."

Bill called our son Trent down from his room and delivered the terrible news to him. The police officer agreed to drive Trent to the hospital to be with his sister. Bill raced out the door and sped off to Sunnybrook, and made phone call after phone call to our family members to share the horrible news. Family members pooled in to support all of us, including Trent who was at his sister's bedside. Once Sydney was released, my sister-in-law and niece drove Trent and Sydney to join their Dad at the hospital to be with me. When they arrived they were greeted by their Dad and their older sister, Sara. By this time there were approximately forty other family members in the cafeteria. After Bill described the state I was in and what to expect, he brought Sara, Trent, and Sydney in to see me for the first time.

I was in a coma for almost three weeks. My family was told my waking was not a guarantee, and if I did wake up my recovery was a mystery. I could be paralyzed, not remember them or any number of things depending on what part of my brain was damaged. The injury I sustained resulted in small bleeds in multiple areas of my brain, so my recovery was questionable.

As I began to come to, I was in a lot of pain and was unable to feel the left side of my body. My neck was in pain, as was my shoulder. I was unable to reposition myself to become more comfortable as I was too weak to lift my own weight. When my family wanted to take me outdoors the nurses had to move me with a lift to a wheelchair. My neck was so weak from the trauma that they had to support my neck with a brace so that it could be held up. It was traumatic for my children to see the strong, independent mother they knew in a state so weak and utterly dependent on others for everything.

I became child-like, begging and pleading for things that I wanted, speaking bluntly and inappropriately about my likes and dislikes, having an inability to express anything other than the truth, and crying multiple times per day. My children were horrified when I would tell them, "I don't like her," while pointing at a nurse. They couldn't believe the proper woman they knew, their mother, was behaving this way.

I suffered a traumatic brain injury. We don't often hear how individuals change after this type of injury. The changes have been lasting and I don't know if I will ever regain control of my emotions, if my ability to retain information, or retrieve information will ever return, or if the ability to keep my attention and focus will improve. I don't know if my vocal cords will ever heal completely, or if I will ever regain my balance and physical strength. The unknowns and the unanswerable questions have been tortuous, for someone who has always strived to be in control and know what to expect.

After 45 years, the brain has trouble adapting to these new inabilities, so they do not register easily. Day after day, when I had to go to the bathroom, I argued with family members that I could do it on my own, as I always had. I was relentless in my will to do what I had always done, and would try to pull myself out of bed multiple times a day. I begged them to help me before they inevitably wrestled me back to bed while explaining that I didn't have the strength or balance to stand without support, let alone to walk. One day, the day before I left for Toronto Rehab I was left alone, which was a rare occurrence. Bill felt it was safe to leave me while I was sleeping to run to the cafeteria to get a snack. I awoke while he was gone and had to go to the washroom. I felt it would be perfectly acceptable to get myself to the bathroom, clearly not remembering the many times Bill had coached me to press the button and call a nurse if I needed help. I managed to pull myself to a standing position and proceeded to the bathroom. At this point, I had not sat up or stood on my own for five weeks, so naturally, after two steps, I hit the floor and knocked myself out.

I've had to learn how to surrender to all of this. Every day I am healing. I have to let go of the idea that I will return to my "old self," and the way I lived my life in the past. I must constantly remind myself not to look back, but only to look forward, and to be grateful for how far I have come on this healing journey.

"Family is a life jacket in the stormy sea of life."
J.K. Rowling

For as long as I can remember, I dreamed of becoming a mother. I have always known my gifts in life would serve me and that I could give children my whole heart and unparalleled devotion. I knew having children would give my life meaning and fulfillment, beyond what I had experienced during the first 25 years of my life, and I'd been certain this was my calling. Indeed I was right, motherhood has given my life rich meaning and has fulfilled me in every way.

I've always been highly sensitive, intuitive, introverted, patient, and kind. I'm also a perfectionist, and I have always set very high standards for myself, which have led to my ever present need to be in complete control over everything, including my emotions, parenting, and all other aspects of my life. I would never expect or ask for help with anything, because I believed it implied weakness, and dependence. I've worked very hard to be a perfect mother and I've been extremely hard on myself. I've often berated any move I saw as less than perfect and not in the best interest of my precious angels. Even the rare occasion of raising my voice has been something that I have judged as poor parenting.

This level of perfectionism has been simply exhausting. When it came to my family, I demanded perfection for everything. I was constantly analyzing every decision and beating myself up over any "mistake." I worked so hard to give them an idyllic childhood. I did not even allow myself to have a bad day. If they had a bad day my heart ached and I suffered silently alongside them, feeling responsible for it in some way. If I had a bad day, I did everything in my power to hide it from them, not wanting to burden them, or for anyone to see me experience any negative feelings. I continuously strived to control my expression of feelings, to appear stoic, to never reveal my true feelings. I never left them for more than a night, with the exception of an annual short trip with their father. I felt that anything longer was unnecessary stress for them and flying anywhere on a couples vacation was simply out of the question. I felt it was too risky. *What if the plane crashed and we died?* I couldn't take that chance!

My children needed me and I was not going to let them down! I measured my worth by how independent and perfect I was at being a mother and taking care of my family. The accident propelled me into a new state of being, as the same woman, with the same values and passions, yet without the ability to remain independent, in control and to strive for perfection.

The new me requires help with basic tasks, such as cooking, cleaning, grocery shopping, navigation, driving, and organizing my daily schedule. I have been blessed with a second chance! An opportunity to JUST BE ME; flawed and imperfect. The new me cannot hold back tears or resist speaking the truth and the new me relies on loved ones for help and support to pursue basic tasks. This is the me that is ok for the first time with being an imperfect version of myself. In fact I'm more real than I have ever been. My near death experience has brought me to an authentic place. I have shifted from being in constant fear and working hard to control everything to now embracing life.

This physical, spiritual and emotional transformation is not the only aspect of my new life vision. What was once a horrific experience, has actually unveiled other valuable truths for me to be more attentive to. Living through what I have lived through has given me an interesting peak at who would be there for my loved ones if I was not; in other words, who would be at my funeral and beyond.

I am very blessed to have had this life experience and the lessons I have learned. I am blessed with the community that surrounds me, including the family and friends who came to help pick up the pieces after our accident. There were numerous friends and family members who came to share love, support, and prayers. These friends walked our dogs, took care of our cats, and my daughter's horse. These friends brought food, drove my kids to and from the hospital, and cleaned our house. They gave us constant love and support. They prayed for me. Each and every one of these precious humans have a place in my heart forever. Each of these individuals are ALL my family, regardless of our bloodlines, they were my lifeline. I have the rest of my life to love and appreciate all those who have been there for us.

So what has brought me to this realization of living my life more authentically, and being less hard on myself, accepting myself with all of my flaws and weaknesses? Well you see, I had a rare opportunity to live in a childlike state and to see that I still had the love of all of my family and friends. I still had their love and support when I said inappropriate things, continually made messes, and required help with absolutely everything. I had to learn to accept help which I had never done before. I have learned that as much as I have to fight through feeling like a burden, that people gain something in this exchange, and that relationships deepen through this. Accepting help when needed is allowing others to give you a gift.

I had to let go of my old ways of constantly working and making sure I was making a contribution that I felt was adequate. *Adequate in who's eyes?* Mine of course. *Adequate for what you ask?* I think in the end it was feeling like a contributing member of my family and my community in order to feel worthy of love. I now see I am worthy of love not for what I contribute or how perfect my life is, but just for being me. I am now learning to let go of who I WAS, and to love THE NEW ME just as I am.

I think of all the years I was looking for something, something better, the more perfect version of myself and now I have to learn to accept who I am now. The new me with a catastrophic brain injury, that can't get a lot done because of my chronic fatigue. The me that is not as physically strong, and has a poor memory. The new me that laughs and cries more. I now realize that what I was looking for was inside of me all along. I may not be able to run around and get so many things accomplished, but my heart has grown and my compassion has deepened. The work I will continue to do is to be gentle with myself, to take my foot off the gas pedal and just embrace my whole self with love, along with the flaws.

"Surrender is a journey from outer turmoil to inner peace."
Sri Chinmoy

Dear Shannon,

You have been given this tough life experience not as a punishment, but as a life lesson. Do everything you can to surrender to it and learn all that you can. The challenges you face in life are always there to serve you on your soul's evolution. Overcoming these and other challenges are what makes your life meaningful.

You have lived your life with the misconception that you had control over everything. This accident didn't happen TO you, it happened FOR you. It is your soul's sacred contract to learn how to be an authentic human and 'just be you', so share your message. Share the message that you are enough, just the way you are. Each individual trying to attain perfection, looking for something better is wasting time. Say I love you to yourself every day. You have so much love for so many, but what about the little girl in you, she longs to be loved too.

You spent 45 years believing that if you did everything in your power to keep yourself safe along with those you love safe, then everything would be ok. But this is 'living in fear' and you miss out on a lot of life experiences in order to "stay safe." This is a sad existence and has limited your life. Life is short! Live each day as though it could be your last, because it could.

'Just Be You' because there is no other person on the planet just like you, so let your light shine! It is easy getting caught up being hard on yourself and comparing yourself to others, but this is a recipe for an unhappy life, so celebrate who you are. Who are you? You are love, kindness, compassion; a mothering, gentle, non-violent soul. This brain injury has allowed you to see your true soul, the true person who has not yet been valued or appreciated.

Tell those you love what they mean to you as often as possible. Do not hold grudges, free yourself of those shackles; not forgiving others does not hurt them, it hurts you. Speak what is on your mind. This brain injury has enabled you to truly see people, to speak the truth, to be authentic and truthful about everything. You worked so hard to always be put together, stoic, and tough, holding back tears, but how about just being real?

You lived your life believing that to be loved and to be worthy of love you had to reach an unattainable level of perfection. But this is untrue and leads to burnout, and disconnect. Do others really know who you truly are when you appear to have it all together but there is a storm inside of you from all the times you do not speak your truth? Who is judging you anyway? You are enough just the way you are. You are worthy of love! You need to accept love from others, as much as you give love to others.

Be in the here and now, stop looking back. It does not serve you! Release guilt and blame, stop beating yourself up. Look yourself in the mirror and say, "I love you" every day. Don't spend another moment buying into the belief that you need to have control.

When we ask the universe or pray to god to heal us or end our suffering please remember that the hardships are part of the healing. They are an essential part of this journey called life, and part of your soul's evolution.

Shannon

Finding a Reason Before Death Finds Me

DEVLYN SARAH

UNFIT FOR THE WORLD

It's been six years since my first diagnosis.

I was just shy of my eleventh birthday when my world went up in flames. An inferno of pain swallowed me whole, leaving no trace of the naïve child that once existed. Survival of the fittest leaves no room for innocence.

For a while, I held desperately onto the hope that one day when the flame's last ember had burnt out, the shell I had become would refill with my lost innocence. However, no person has the power to return a lost childhood, let alone the prior existing unscathed child with it.

I sit here now just shy of my seventeenth birthday; a shell of the child I used to be. I know now being tightly tucked into bed cannot protect me from the monsters in this world. Especially since the monsters I've met thus far have not resided under my bed.

I can't recall the moment I realized that the little girl I once was would not be returning. Maybe it wasn't a specific moment, but rather a number of events that eventually broke my rose-coloured glasses beyond repair.

I never had the time to mourn. I was so busy making sure I actually didn't die, that mourning the innocence I lost seemed insignificant. If I'm being honest, I also didn't wish to let go. It might seem weird to some that I needed to mourn. No death actually occurred yet never again would that prior me ever live. All people change as they grow older and experience life, but my descent into adulthood happened seemingly overnight. Most people will have traces of their young self hidden in their older identity, but I don't.

It was also my child self's dreams that I feel I have to mourn. I was a planner before the pain. I had my whole future planned out. I would graduate high school with straight A's, go to university for orthodontia and eventually open my own practice. As for my personal life, I would marry the man of my dreams, have two kids (an older boy and a younger girl) and having had grown up with dogs, *of course* I pictured one in my future.

I didn't plan for the pain or the disorders. I couldn't have imagined what had happened. Sure, I had dealt with death and bullying but, my optimistic self could never have envisioned the events that would soon unfold. Sometimes, I still have trouble believing that what has occurred has actually happened. Especially since it has happened in such a short period of time. I know it has happened though because the physical, mental and emotional scars never let me forget.

It seems comical at times that I'm not even seventeen, yet I have seven diagnoses. Laughing instead of crying has become one of my coping strategies over these past years. It helps me disassociate from the pain I was forced to endure at such a young and tender age.

I had to learn to survive when I was still a child. I didn't deserve what happened to me. Nothing any child does makes them worthy of feeling the hopelessness that I felt, that was caused by the events I've experienced. Despite being undeserving of such pain, I lost my childhood to my disorders and their stressors.

One of the problems I faced with developing disorders at age eleven was that I didn't know who I was yet. I had no identity, so when my life became panic attacks, multiple doctor visits and medication changes, my diagnoses became my identity. I believed for many years that I could be summed up in a few short lines written by my latest psychiatrist.

I received my first diagnosis when I was eleven. Since that time, I have received the other six that make up the seven. I figure the easiest way to understand my experience of each disorder and the order in which they were diagnosed is for me to list them with a quick synopsis of the feelings that each disorder brings. Then explain the events that made the disorders develop in my brain. Please be aware that my mental illnesses were not developed from happy situations. To understand my growth and where I am now, my past must first be understood.

1. Heart palpitating, head pounding and I'm drowning in the *what if's?* (Generalized Anxiety Disorder)

2. I can feel the heat of their scrutinizing leers and I can't seem to shrink into myself enough to lessen the weight of them staring. I avoid that place, in fact I avoid all places. (Social Anxiety Disorder)

3. My patterns and obsessions don't make sense to them. Their emotions don't make sense to me and I'm looking at their foreheads again to avoid eye contact. (Autism Spectrum Disorder)

4. All I want to do is sleep, but I can't. I'm numb. Even the blade doesn't work anymore. I despise the thing that stares back at me in the mirror. I just need it all to stop. (Major Depressive Disorder)

5. I'm spinning, literally. My vision is closing in and I can't see or think straight. The only way to make it stop is to sleep a minimum of 8 hours and take proper care of myself nutritionally. However, taking care of my basic needs is challenging because of my self-defeating behaviours. (Migraine Disorder)

6. I can't remember most of the event. My dissociative amnesia tries to protect me from the horror I faced in a place that was supposed to help me. However, even with the amnesia it still took years to go into a doctor's office and not feel like the walls were closing in on me. It took years to not view a needle as a punishment or not think each pill I swallowed could be my eradication. (Illness Induced PTSD)

7. His words haunt me. I can't shake the feeling of utter worthlessness he built into me. I can't help, but hate myself for being so weak. I will never again see a person and not wonder what damage they could do. The insomnia causes more panic and when I do crash from exhaustion, I awake with tears streaming down my face in the midst of a panic attack. (Complex PTSD)

My anxiety disorders were diagnosed at the same time. While they may have developed from my autism, they were so severe that they each needed their own diagnosis. It started small; in kindergarten my teacher told my mom that I was an anxious child. Every report card stated it took me many months to become comfortable. At eleven my hormones seemed to kick my anxiety into overdrive. I was having multiple panic attacks daily. I quit all extracurricular activities and eventually I couldn't attend school. My social anxiety caused me to be homebound and terrified of the outside world. My perfectionism skyrocketed. I believed wholeheartedly that everyone was constantly judging me. A hair out of place would cause me an uncontrollable panic attack.

Soon after my twelfth birthday I was diagnosed with Autism, specifically I have Asperger's although that is no longer seen as a separate diagnosis. It was hard for me to pick up on social cues. I wasn't interested in what my peers enjoyed. My obsessions were severe. I could talk for hours without care if the person I was around enjoyed the topic. I became a pro at hiding my abnormalities. My mask of normalcy was worn daily. However, it tired me out. Recuperation took hours.

The depression diagnosis came later when I was fourteen. I had hidden it for many years. I was highly suicidal and it showed through cutting, skin picking and head banging. At times I had to be watched around the clock by my parents. I couldn't be trusted. I wished for death and the nothingness it entailed. One of the hardest moments was telling my mom. I had to tell the woman that birthed me that I didn't want to live the life she gave me. The self hatred and wish for death were unescapable.

My Migraine Disorder was an accountability creator. If I did not force myself to live healthily, I would randomly lose my vision and crash to the floor multiple times a day followed by an intense headache.

When I was eleven, I was put on a medication called Prozac. I became uncontrollable. I was maniacal during panic attacks. My parents could no longer control me as the behaviours escalated. They brought me to a hospital and there I was admitted on a form one in a psych ward. My fear of needles came from being strapped to a bed while injected with a sedative. Following this I was left overnight, unable to move from the restraints. I spent the next three days alone and afraid. My parents were not allowed to visit. I had some-one stationed outside of my room at night because I was seen as a threat. I was heartbroken; time ran together in the psych ward and I believed my parents had abandoned me. On the second last day I asked for support and yet again as per usual they gave me more pills. The pill I was given was called Haldol; it caused a dystonic reaction. Typically, this reaction isn't life threatening however, I had one in my larynx. It caused asphyxiation. I was being suffocated to death. The only thing I remember is the pain. It hurt more to breathe than not. I had to force myself to take each shallow gasp of air knowing that every breath felt like I was swallowing fire. My throat was seizing as were other parts of my body, yet I could only focus on my breath and try to win the fight to stay conscious. I knew that if I didn't keep breathing in that moment, I wouldn't get to breathe again. I survived. I had to again, be stabbed with a needle that undid the damage they caused. My last memory of the psych ward was on the third day. My assigned staff member told me that my parents were right through a set of doors. I was overjoyed. I wanted to go home. I ran to those doors and just as I was about to push them open that staff member told me that if I went through those doors, she would keep me there. I broke even more in that moment.

My Complex PTSD stemmed from emotional, mental and physical abuse. My brother had taken to drugs and alcohol. He became violent and angry, screaming at me for hours on end. I became terrified of being in my own home. He manipulated my love for him to make me cover up his addiction. I lied about many things ranging from the holes in the walls to what he had said to me. My own brother who I had once seen as my hero threatened to kill me. He would push me around and hit me. The emotional abuse was far worse though, in fact he once even told me to go back to the psych ward. When he was abusing substances, he was narcissistic. He enjoyed seeing me in pain and knowing he put me there. This lasted for many years and even when he did become sober, he would never admit to the abuse.

WALLS CRUMBLING DOWN

Say goodbye to the fourteen because they are never coming back.

Do you not understand?

I didn't for a long time. Forty seconds seemed like an insignificant amount of time compared to the amount of time in a day. It seems miniscule compared to the days, weeks, months or years each person has left on this earth. Except for those fourteen. They stopped their clock.

No less than fourteen people committed suicide in the time it took for you to read my backstory. This is important to me. It matters to me because I could have been one of the many to have lost their fight. Honestly, I had a higher chance of committing suicide then I had of surviving. I remind myself of this fact daily. My survival was not pretty. It was grueling and ugly. I have gone to over 70 health care specialists to find people that could help me. The amount of medication I have tried is insane. At times I felt like a science experiment. I found many more dead ends than I did roads, to mental stability.

I worked tirelessly to try to ensure I would be alive for another day. Most often I didn't live for myself. I lived so that my mom wouldn't find my body and my dad wouldn't have to think *"what if?"* I lived so that my non abusive brother wouldn't have to explain to my nephew why I couldn't play with him anymore or tell my baby niece who the girl was in his wedding photos.

I refuse to apologize for what I had to do to live. Everyone's method of surviving is different. Sadly, some people don't find theirs in time. And I can't blame the fourteen for wanting the pain to stop. In fact, I recognize why they had to and *yes*, I say *had to*, because at that point, there is no other option that can be seen. This is coming from someone who has been at that point several times and has written many goodbyes. I won't say that I was lucky to survive. I was just one of the few who found a reason before death found me. I was asked once, to promise, to never cut again. The person that said this, said it out of love for me, but I told them that I wouldn't make a promise I knew I couldn't keep. For a long time cutting helped me survive and I'm proud that I was able to cut because it meant I didn't kill. I know it's a hard concept to understand and by no means am I condoning self harm. My point is this; no one has the right to tell you how to survive.

HAPPY ENDING — NOT PROMISED

My life is a trigger warning. Even now, when I'm at a point in my life that I can truthfully call myself happy, traumas still surround me. I'd be lying if I said I'm happy constantly because that isn't life. Some days I still think that tomorrow isn't meant for me. I'd be lying if I said I will never cut again. While I have been clean for months, I realize something might happen that causes me to relapse. And as I'm writing this my wrists are tingling because I can still feel the blade swiping across my skin. It still itches because I can remember the feeling after the cuts scabbed. I doubt I will ever be able to think of moments like when I cut and not experience the sensations I felt. Just like the physical scars the emotional and mental ones will never leave me. I never want anyone to hear my story and see who I am now and think, "Wow, I want to experience that so I can be like her."

I went through hell and I will remember it as such. I have been told for years how "mature" I am for my age and I still get angry hearing this because nothing that I have gained from the horrors that I have gone through makes me delusional enough to forget how I gained them. I have earned everything I have now. My past is something I wouldn't wish on anyone. This doesn't mean I can't love where I am now and it doesn't stop me from working on loving who I am now. What it means is that even though I am now able to live instead of just survive, it doesn't mean my pain is gone.

It doesn't mean I will never again experience more horrors. My life isn't perfect now. It is so far from it and always will be. Life isn't perfect. I still wake up in cold sweats sometimes and still think other people are weirdly staring at me in public. I still hate making eye contact. However, I have gained the skills that allow me to enjoy the life I've earned. While I'm a shell of who I used to be, I am a complete person of who I am now.

Here's to many more breakdowns and breakthroughs.

This has been an interesting trip down memory lane and I guess a eulogy for the girl I used to be and an appreciation for who I have become.

Divine Love

DANIELLE ROSA

A CALL TO BE MORE

She received a phone call and heard the voice on the other end, "Jackie is gone."

She found out her best friend took her own life.

A new phase in her life had just begun, and it was the passing of her loved ones.

She didn't know at the time, but death was her messenger.

Death allowed her to deliberately focus.

Death was how she finally learned the meaning of true LOVE.

A topic that everyone around her avoided. But to her, death became a place to find her clarity.

It allowed her to feel with no reservation.

It showed her what she was made of.

It allowed her to find true purpose in life and most of all, it showed the true POWER that was within her all along.

SIFTING AND SORTING

I was a regular kid enjoying life but learning from the ones around me that things were supposed to be difficult and full of struggle, sacrifice and suffering. I started seeing more and more evidence of that, and I started to believe it.

In my eyes, my family was hurting spiritually, emotionally, mentally and physically.

I wanted better for myself and felt that no one seemed to care or really understand.

The older I got, the more independent I became. It felt good to be in control and make things 'happen' for myself.

My belief was that by working hard, my life would eventually get better for me, and it did; but it wasn't sustainable.

I worked three jobs and was putting myself through college, but I felt resentful for it.

On the outside, others saw me as being smart, bright, put-together and having a good head on my shoulders. Within, it felt like a constant struggle to motivate myself and continue forward to the end goal of finally being happy.

My earliest memory of wanting happiness was while on vacation in Portugal with my aunt. She asked me "if you had only one wish in life, what would it be?" and I replied, "to be happy."

It was important to me to be happy and what I pictured it to look like was: a beautiful home, a loving family, happy relationships, a healthy body, financial freedom just to name a few.

I didn't know how to attain happiness from where I was.

I read every self help book that felt relevant to me at any given moment.

I would stay in my room, creating and enjoying my space that I had complete control over. It was my sanctuary and this is where my love for interior design began.

I would spend the rest of my time at my friends' houses where I felt better. I admired their families and appreciated how they lived in comfortable, beautiful homes, and got along with one another. This to me portrayed happiness.

I continued to invest in myself, opening my mind to new perspectives which allowed me to feel like I had more control of my life.

I chose to go to college and invest in my passion for Interior Design. I loved the feeling of being in beautiful spaces and saw the benefit it brought to me and others. I linked happiness with beautiful spaces because my own home wasn't that way.

MIND OVER MATTER

By the time I was in 2nd year of college, my life was full of stress; pulling all nighters just to stay on top of my school work deadlines, working every day to pay for school and trying to be the best aspiring designer I needed to be in order to be successful.

I wasn't the only one stressed to the max. My best friend was also having a challenging time juggling school life, work, personal and family situations.

While at work one Saturday morning, I received a phone call from my best friends' brother and heard him say "Jackie is gone."

My best friend had chosen to end her life.

I was devastated and appalled to say the least.

My life came to a halt and I had no idea where to look next. I needed something to heal the pain. Life and school was still in full effect. Although I spent many days in grief and trying to find relief at home, it felt best to go back to school and focus on something else altogether. I informed my teachers and head program coordinator of what had recently happened and with a quick and loving nudge, I started my first counselling session with the college social worker.

I needed answers, anything that would help me feel better and understand what was going on and find clarity on what my life had now become. She asked me mind opening questions and listened without judgment. She asked how my best friend must have been feeling in order to do something to that extent. She asked how my best friend wanted me to move forward without her.

It was all so helpful. Bit by bit, I slowly gained my balance back. The more sessions I had with her, the more I felt secure and clearer about myself and my life.

I remember feeling so thankful that this kind of support and wisdom was available to me as it became a profound pivotal moment in my life. I realized her role was to shine a light on what I was wanting to feel and discover for myself, and she did exactly that.

Through our sessions, I came to realize that no matter what I say or what I do, I have no 'real' control over anyone's decision of what they choose for themselves. It was freeing to feel and know the truth in that because I had experienced that many times before with people I cared for, including my best friend.

Before her death I tried talking to my best friend through a better perspective (looking for the positives in her situation). I tried everything that I thought that could help her feel better, loved and hopeful that everything was going to be okay, but I couldn't control what she chose to think on her own. I didn't know what she was really feeling or thinking.

I realized that I assumed I knew what she was going through. I thought I could change her focus, but didn't understand how this could happen to her or me until much later.

There were many moments of me not believing that this was now my reality and that my best friend was no longer here in the physical. But the more I continued to have sessions with my counselor, the more I could remember how important it was to feel good, by thinking and looking for a positive perspective, it became my addiction. The more I focused that way, the longer I could hold it and the easier it got to continue moving forward with life.

With this new and empowered understanding of taking responsibility of my own choices, focus, thoughts and actions;

and trusting others to know and do the same for themselves, I felt relief. It was the relief I had been looking for. Freedom from the bondage of taking ownership of how others felt and having the freedom to choose how I wanted to feel.

It took some time to practice this new way of thinking. It felt lighter to me which kept me looking for that feeling more and more.

It was a significant shift and bit by bit, it got easier to sustain this new way of thinking and I could see more clearly that I had a choice to feel better if I looked for it. Looking for that feeling of relief felt uplifting and empowering to me and I never wanted to go back to anything less.

A year after my best friend passed, my mom was diagnosed with stage 4 cancer. The doctors informed us that there were no treatments, surgeries or medications that would diminish it just like the first time she had it eight years prior.

My mother was not one to talk much. She kept to herself and whenever I asked her for her advice, because I thought as an adult and a mother, she would know better for me; instead she would always put it back onto me. She always told me that I had the answers and I knew what was best for myself. I didn't understand, until much later, what she was really trying to tell me.

My mother displayed great power and resilience throughout her journey of 'DIS'ease.

When the doctors gave her an estimated three to six months left to live, she went on bypassing it over three years.

When the doctors put her on oxygen support and told her she had to stay at the hospital because she was too weak, she was released within one week, breathing on her own because she wanted to be at home.

She showed me that when she focused deliberately on something, she got what she wanted.

She was powerful and it was all within her mind.

After she passed, I gathered these golden pieces from my life and I began to see the importance of my everyday environment in order to move forward.

In order to tend to the feelings of ease and clarity and to maintain my emotional balance, it was easier to have my own space that I knew was mostly going to be calm and consistent.

I moved out of my family home into a small basement apartment.

It helped and my life became more and more full and abundant. I started my own business in Interior Design, learned about Feng Shui, started meeting influential and wonderful people, feeling satisfied in my relationships and having more fun.

Life was better. I was gaining momentum towards happiness.

I made a decision to focus on what I wanted and promised myself that I could find a way to make it happen.

I received an opportunity to move onto bigger and more exciting projects through my work and things went into fast-mode.

All the things I had been wanting to achieve like my dream job, travelling, more financial support, and a sense of control and freedom in my life came into full fruition.

It was glorious and I would catch myself often saying, "I'm living my dream."

My life was moving quickly and it was all exhilarating to me. I was up to speed with it all and ready for more. The more details that came, the more delicious and satisfying it was.

Simply looking at my current lifestyle of designing beautiful homes with lovely clients, traveling for work and leisure, supporting myself financially with ease just made me happier. I expected it to stay the same and continue to fulfill me, but it did not.

Just like everything in life, my personal preferences, my relationships, my work was becoming more. New things I wanted to experience from the place I was standing were calling me to refocus on what I now preferred.

Then the thrill of my current life became less satisfying and the new desires became stronger and louder. I didn't know how to keep up and I started to feel tired and needed more rest but my work, relationships, and responsibilities needed my attention.

My belief of 'work hard and make things happen' was still in full effect and I didn't know how to find balance dealing with my new dreams calling me.

As the days continued, the gut wrenching feeling within me of being unhappy with my life, hit me again.

I didn't know at the time, but my main focus was on the things happening around me, and when they started showing faults to me, they just got bigger and eventually got the best of me.

My belief of working hard didn't support the flexibility and replenishment I needed to evolve and flow with my new desires, which meant I had to rely on my practiced habits of pushing through the negative emotions, making decisions and taking action when I didn't feel good just to 'make' my dreams work out for me.

My dreams, happiness, and ideal outcomes required a refined focus of what I wanted rather than what I didn't want.

I needed more practices to sustain and understand my emotional balance that I didn't have nor knew about at the time.

Things continued to decline in my energy and later found myself fighting with others who I normally connected with. I felt discouraged in my work all together which led to me doubting myself, my career, and relationships.

CONNECTING THE DOTS

It had been four years since my mom had passed when I received a call one night that my dad had passed away from a heart attack.

"Here we go again," I heard myself say.

I've been through this before, but I felt a big gap from where I was and where I wanted to be in my life.

I thought I had done all the hard work already and it would stick.

Wouldn't this now be easier for me? I thought to myself.

This was another transcending opportunity for me.

I thought I had it all figured out; life would all fall into place from the lessons and new perspectives I had come to know up until this point.

I was called to go deeper within myself and do what I already knew worked for me in the moment until I figured this new way out.

I focused on actions that felt good, I took space and time to myself, I cried when I felt like it, I fed myself, and rested whenever I needed to.

It helped a bit, but there was a sense of deeper relief I needed, a more lasting relief.

I had to focus more on feeling my way to better feelings rather than thinking the right thought or doing the right actions. It was challenging because my current life had become one of thinking, doing, and pushing.

I was then laid off from my job which gave me the time to slow down on daily tasks, feel my way through the day, be on my own schedule and tend to my needs with the financial support from unemployment. It wasn't the long term solution, but it helped.

I remember feeling the importance of my focus, putting my attention on what felt brighter or lighter to me in the moment. I had to look forward because everything around me felt heavy and stuck.

Settling our estate was a pressing task that needed immediate attention before I was ready, so I had to break it up into small parts in order to grasp the situation or simply have the energy to focus. I was required to work with multiple family members, all with strong and different opinions, who I would usually not discuss important life decisions with as I was so used to relying on myself, but the estate was an urgent matter and involved many people. Settling it was my only guiding light.

There were so many moving parts that it felt like my life forced me to be gentle on myself and the others because anything else felt terrible to withstand.

We all needed to work together where my immediate habit to take control of the situation myself and direct others needed to take a backseat.

I needed to work from a place of kindness, understanding and compassion for others. It is what allowed things to run smoothly and calmly and mostly, it felt better for me.

Step by step, more things got done and the journey was more fulfilling to be a part of. Feelings of clarity, understanding and appreciation started coming to me more often.

This emotional shift allowed me to feel more optimistic about the future.

The estate was settled and we all could now move forward with more ease and opportunities than ever before.

The ease and opportunities came in many forms; knowledge, confidence in myself, better relationships with my family, a new career path and more financial ease to allow my interests and passions to be supported.

Finances were a great factor in my sense of freedom and happiness. As mentioned previously; in my eyes, my family struggled a lot and mainly because the focus was on money. As I now had more money than ever before, I felt free and finally I could be happy, well at least that's what I thought.

Then the questions came:

Why did I always seem to thrive in these situations?

Why did these significant moments of great loss allow such great clarity and results at the end?

I invested my time and money into this new discovery.

A refreshing and bigger focus was calling.

I wanted to help others receive the same success in their challenging situations.

I enrolled in a coaching program, travelled and lived abroad, and did everything that made my heart sing. As I quickly discovered, many people I connected with had many challenging situations and they were all so different than mine.

I shared my practices and mindset, but their outcomes were not as significant as I felt they 'should' be.

More profound questions came.

How could I and others achieve success in any situation and maintain happiness daily?

How could I help others find the answers within themselves?

How could I stay stable in my clarity and knowledge of who I am and who others really are?

These questions led to great revelations.

It led me to the universal laws and understanding of how life really works and how it applies to all situations for all people.

LOVE in its purest sense, was the simple answer and it was the only thing that connected us all.

More discovery was required.

I learned more about vibration and energy and how it's all connected to our focus, thoughts and emotions.

It all clicked together for me.

My personal experiences on how I felt in each significant moment of my life, was explained within this universal law.

This perspective, teaching and practice has transformed my understanding of how life works and how to feel better in any moment no matter where I stand.

Focusing where it felt good was the key.

Finding a way to feel better in the moment is where my power was found.

This simple formula of looking for a better feeling thought whenever I stood somewhere I didn't like, was what allowed me to move forward in love; enjoy my journey and have conditions work out in satisfying ways.

The insight my mother shared with me, about having all the answers within me, I'm now able to fully understand.

How you feel is all that matters and feeling good is more powerful than any words or actions you can ever offer anyone who you are wanting to help.

From your place of being happy (feeling good), you speak words of LOVE, you act in LOVE, and you are a part of the solutions to all your problems and those you love too.

So do what feels best for you. Find your better feeling place within your mind, right where you are and know that with just that simple effort, you affect your world immensely and positively.

I'll leave you with this quote that may allow you to feel the resonance within yourself of what may be true and a guiding light for you as it continues to be for me.

"You were born with a magnificent (emotional) guidance system that lets you know, in every moment, exactly what your vibrational content is, which is being matched by the Law of Attraction. As it is your desire to feel good, and your practice to choose good feeling thoughts, only good things will come to you."
Abraham Hicks

What do you stand for?

TINA ADDORISIO

SECRETS

Jack pulled her in closer, hungry for more, as he sensed she was ready to go.

She stumbled around aimlessly collecting her clothes that he had previously peeled off.

"I can't do this anymore! I'm sorry," she babbled to him while putting herself back together.

Panic struck her as she ran to her car. She couldn't run away fast enough. No matter how quick she ran, she couldn't outrun the guilt.

Kate! You gave into temptation AGAIN, she scolded herself in shame.

She felt sad. Things were getting out of control.

After pulling into her driveway, she sent Ben a text, "Just got in from work. I'll call you in five!"

Ring ring.

"Hey! How was your day?"

Ben shared a story from his day and then with concern asked, "Why are they keeping you so late at work? You must be exhausted!"

"They're restructuring their systems and need extra support," Kate stuttered while secretly wiping her tears.

The truth was that she wasn't exhausted from working long hours.

She was exhausted from hiding.

Jack was her escape. He fed into her need for connection, variety and feeling significant. His hunger for Kate kept her returning for more.

Ben and Kate started dating in their teens.

Soon after the honeymoon phase, everything went downhill.

They put a lot of time and energy into their separate hobbies, friends and work. By days end, they had nothing left for each other. They were bored. He wasn't open to trying new things and Kate nagged him about his choice of friends.

Kate and Ben were growing apart and neither of them had the courage to address that breaking up was the next logical step.

It was easier to avoid the conversation. They weren't ready to face the truth.

Kate was exhausted from playing out the exit options in her head.

Anxiety filled her chest and shallowed her breathing.

Ben and Kate had made many promises to each other about their future. The dream home, the marriage and children; they promised all of it. The more time Kate spent seeking pleasure outside of their relationship, the more stuck she felt. She couldn't see a way out. She was terrified.

While quietly keeping their true feelings inside, weeks turned into months and months turned into years. They were living separate lives.

Kate loved her yoga practice. The more time she spent on her mat, the closer she got to understanding why she chose unfaithfulness over communication.

She had been a people pleaser since she was a child and feared others' opinions.

Ben was a great guy. He checked off all the boxes. Many friends reminded her that he was a *great catch.* The opinions mattered and left her in doubt.

One night after yoga, she heard a wailing voice inside her head, *LEAVE. You can't go on living a secret life! It's not who you are!*

Kate was a woman of integrity and her actions were revealing that she was in a state of distress. She needed help.

She feared her reputation. If anyone found out about her escape, she'd be mortified.

She was the hardest on herself, constantly criticizing her actions. Being involved with Jack went against her core values.

Kate was always acknowledged as a caring person that would never cross the line. Following the rules was seen as a big part of her character, and because this was a quality that was often praised, she feared losing people's respect.

No one knew how unhappy she was because Kate didn't trust many with her feelings.

Every single time she cheated on Ben, she felt sick to her stomach, *Is this really happening?* she'd think.

One day, while at work, she had an emotional breakdown and left.

She wanted to come clean and tell someone about her imperfections and faults.

"I have secrets," she confessed to her coach.

"These secrets are eating me alive and I don't know what to do anymore!"

Kate's coach saw how the guilt, shame and regret were impacting her well being. She helped her see that Ben wasn't the only person she was cheating on.

"Kate. You're cheating *yourself*. When was the last time you said yes because you *wanted* to say yes?"

Kate couldn't recall a time. She even realized that her time with Jack wasn't what she really wanted.

She wanted to start over.

For the first time in months, she felt clearer. She found hope in believing that being happy was possible. Before buying into the collective stigma of, once a cheater always a cheater, she was willing to give herself another chance.

The one person she had the most control over was the person she wanted to gain control over; herself.

Ben and Kate finally had the tough conversations they were avoiding. They were in disagreement about many important things involving their future, which confirmed that they were on different paths. Their breakup left them heartbroken.

THE SIGNS

Breakups are NOT easy, but they are necessary.

The *happily ever after* movies many of us watch don't display the reality of what happens when relationships end. The uncertainty creates a lot of fear in people which keeps them stuck and unhappy.

What will others think?

What will others say?

Caring about the answer to these questions creates a belief that our power belongs to those around us. This is limiting.

Kate's transformation took flight when she realized that a) she was cheating on Ben *and* herself and b) her power and courage came from within, not from outside sources.

As the author of this chapter, it's time I properly introduce myself.

I'm Tina.

I chose to write about integrity because as most of you may have already guessed, Kate's story mirrors times in my past.

A big part of my growth, came from the hiccups of being disloyal and unfaithful. My cheating habits were out of alignment with who I wanted to become. My essence knew better, yet I still participated.

Why do we stay in the relationships we've outgrown?

Why do we say yes, when it's a full bodied no?

Why do we let things happen again, even after promising that it's our last?

We've been trained to please.

We've been trained that putting ourselves first is selfish.

People pleasers place others' thoughts and feelings above their own.

Are you in a people pleasing pattern? If so, you're not alone.

Many of us still care deeply about others' opinions.

Who trained us to please?

With or without awareness, we've watched people in our circles model this behaviour and we've copied them.

It takes a very conscious and mindful individual with heightened awareness, to catch themselves creating a habit that was picked up from an outside source.

How does one break the cycle?

By deciding that you've had enough.

By committing (with a support system) to do everything in your power to follow through until the pattern is broken.

By focusing on your purpose and passions.

And lastly, but most importantly, remembering your pain and using it as your leverage to do whatever it takes to stay focused on your new path.

We have access to the courage life requires from us to make drastic changes. I know this at my core, which is why I can confidently say that *anyone* can break cycles.

Am I proud of my past? Absolutely not.

I hated who I became. Guilt and shame ate me alive every single day.

What I know for sure is that by choosing to make those poor choices, it gifted me the opportunity to lend a guiding hand to those stuck in similar situations.

This reason holds enough meaning for me to transform any residual guilt and shame I have into self compassion.

I made mistakes that hurt others. I was demoralized by what I had caused. I feared it was going to be a long road to finding true love and that my karma was going to sneak up and find me.

STIGMAS

Beyond my realization of needing to feel seen, heard and special from who I was in a relationship with, I also learned that the body is first to reveal when it's out of alignment.

Stress shows up in our skin, weight, hair, nails, digestion, and habits.

It's puzzling that we ignore the signs.

When I wasn't aligned with my integrity, I barely recognized myself in the mirror.

I had cystic acne around my jawline, bulging collarbones, and layers of foundation suffocating my skin.

I overlooked these as signs because it was too distressing to face the truth.

My personal truth was too uncomfortable to accept. Isn't that bizarre?

I was willing to live by the truth of those around me, fitting myself into their tight cocoon, yet all I yearned for was to be a butterfly. I wished to be emancipated from society's views.

In sharing this story, I'm able to clearly see what my blind-spots were.

The first one being the stigmas.

Nice girls don't cheat!

Only men cheat!

Once a cheater, always a cheater!

These beliefs held me hostage. They're false.

What's true is that anyone can fall off path, behave outside of their integrity, and gender has nothing to do with making harmful choices.

All of these stigmas made it hard for me to tell the truth.

I needed professional help to end how I was impacting others *and* myself.

I associated my actions with who I was in a relationship with, but in fact like Kate, it had nothing to do with them. I wasn't living in my integrity and it was because I stopped listening to my heart.

My second blindspot was about needing attention from outside sources. In my relationship I felt unseen, unheard, and overlooked. My desperate attempts in trying to make things right only confirmed that the relationship was coming to an end. In that knowing, I *should've* left.

The part of me that needed certainty wanted to stay. The wise part of me was ready to leave because it knew that the man of my dreams was out there.

The calculated risk was to stay until I was clear that leaving was what I wanted. My mistake was in leaving when it was convenient for me. I did this because I thought it would've saved us both a lot of heartache, but in the end we were both heartbroken because breakups aren't supposed to be easy.

INTEGRITY

If you know your faults, accept your mistakes, show your imperfections, and tell the truth, you'll become an individual that people *can* trust.

You are more than that.

When I admitted that my story was relative to what happened between Ben and Kate, it was to give you permission to give yourself another chance to believe that you *are* trustworthy.

If you've cheated yourself and others, you're not an untrustworthy person. Don't let this experience define your future by accepting a label.

Push against the odds and prove to yourself that you are worthy of *never* putting yourself through that again, nor anyone else.

You were screaming for help through your actions. Plain and simple.

Consider that your mess has a message that can help someone move through their pain. If not right now, at some point.

We all want to skip the painful components of our past, but who we become in the process of working through our stuff *is* the gold. When we arrive to the light at the end of the tunnel, it's so important to maintain a healthy level of reflection of what it took for you to be where you are today. This is your leverage. Your imperfections, faults, and mistakes have become your tools to leverage what you'll never put yourself through again. You have new standards because of your pain. Don't wish it away. Welcome it and turn that sloppy mess into a powerful message.

You now stand for something greater; integrity.

I appreciate where I've been because in my relationship today, we cultivate love and trust through our commitment to love ourselves first. We believe self love is our foundation and it impacts how we show up for each other.

May you forgive yourself and remember that despite who you've hurt along the way, you are still loveable, enough and perfect just as you are.

With light,
Tina

SPECIAL NOTE:
To those of you who've been cheated,

There's nothing anyone can do to change what's been done. You've experienced deep hurt and you have every right to vocalize it how you need. I hope you can digest that their actions had NOTHING to do with you and it's not your fault. People who cheat are unhappy with themselves and don't know how to face their inner demons. It's not your job to fix them. *You* are the most important thing and your happiness matters. I sincerely apologize for the hurt they caused. Whether or not they've given you a sincere apology, I hope you're able to release yourself from the pain. Sending you love.

Breaking the Chains

ASHLEY-ANN PEREIRA

HAPPY NEVER AFTER...?

At the age of three, I lost the man who was supposed to call me "princess."

I wanted him to teach me how to ride a bike and tell me I'm not allowed to date until I'm thirty-five. I was three when my parents went their separate ways. My dad stayed in New Jersey while my mom, sisters and I came back to Toronto. The best part is that I remember nothing about that day. I do remember that one time he came to parent-teacher night while I was in elementary school. I had the chance to introduce him to my friends and I remember feeling so excited and proud to show him off. It felt as though, for once, I could fit in with my friends who had "complete" families. It was my one night to play pretend with my dad. And I also remember the short phone calls and the ones that felt screened by whoever picked up the phone.

For many years, there was a lot that I didn't know, especially about why my parents went their separate ways. I didn't know why we weren't in touch regularly and I didn't understand why there was so much hurt and pain whenever he was brought up in conversation. To be honest, I didn't care that everyone was hurting. I wanted to have a dad and as I heard my friends talking about their dads, it stung. I feared I would never know what it would be like to know my dad.

I was raised while being protected from the truth and thought that not having a dad or "man around the house" was normal.

I grew up seeing my mom struggle.

All on her own, she struggled while raising her three daughters. It was a struggle to pay bills, feed herself, and be present while going from job to job. Can you believe she had three jobs all at the same time?

But I never, not once, felt a lack of love or presence from her. She was always there.

I know it wasn't easy for her, or my older sisters. They carried the weight of providing for the family. I witnessed the three most important people in my life working hard and I couldn't help but feel a responsibility to do the same. I was thirteen-years-old when I was hired for my first part-time job. I was a cashier; a young, petite, and shy grade eight student working at a big grocery store (that's not something you see every day). While my friends made plans to hang out at the park after school, I was rushing home to catch the bus for work.

At a very young age, I felt the need to care for myself. It wasn't because my mom couldn't or wouldn't provide, but it was because her hard work inspired a desire within me to pitch in. The owner of the grocery store was fond of my sisters because they were hard working women which made it easy for me to get the job. My very first job interview was in a grocery store aisle. While enjoying every working minute, I loved earning my own money because I didn't have to feel the wave of guilt from having to ask my mom.

As I look back at my childhood, I see how these years shaped me. I was closed off and scared to let people into my life because I believed that if I did, then I'd become too attached, and eventually they'd leave forever. Just like my dad.

I noticed my attachment to my sisters' boyfriends as they fulfilled the void I had around having a male role model around the house. But as you can imagine, we don't always spend the rest of our lives with our first boyfriend or girl-friend. So when their relationship would end, they would validate the belief I had been repeating to myself over and over. People always leave. And there was absolutely no way I was going to show how heartbroken I was because it didn't change anything. So I bottled up every emotion.

It became nearly impossible for me to trust anyone because at the back of my mind I was wondering how long they were going to be around. At the same time, I learned how to avoid self-expression at all costs.

I was protective of my mom and sisters and often wor-ried about them. Even while not being able to fully trust, I never shied away from dating because I loved to love and feel loved. I didn't realize, though, until I began dating how guarded I was.

I had many relationships and flings throughout my younger days, never lasting longer than eight months. The moment I felt things were getting serious, I'd end the relationship. When there was an argument of any sort, I'd end the relationship. I even had a three strike policy. It was easier to break-up, than try to make things work. Deep down I didn't want to put the effort in because it was easier to leave them, before they left me. I was avoiding heartbreak. For once, it felt good being in control of the outcome, unlike when my dad left.

As I got older, I was free to see things for what they were and create my own beliefs around my parents' separation. My dad became the absent father and while experiencing an abundance of anger, I knew I needed to find a way to accept this reality. It was most obvious when I started telling people that I wanted to change my last name because I felt that he was just a sperm donor. I'd tell anyone that'd listen that I no longer cared about him. Deep down, this behaviour was a cry for his presence, so I could feel loved and wanted. Simply put, I just wanted to know that he cared about me. I imagined that if I received that from him, it would fix the void I felt and all my problems would be washed away. But I knew that until that happened, I could count on myself and this gave me power to move forward.

I didn't believe in happy marriages nor did I believe that I'd find *my person.* It seemed everyone around me was either

separated or divorced, so I created a belief that I had to financially support myself at all costs.

Happily ever after isn't in the cards for me, I'd think and so I
became content with the idea that it would just be me, myself
and I for life. Those were truths and beliefs I created from
my circumstances; they were my holy grail. I became fixated
on the idea that love from my family, friends or a significant
other would make me feel complete.

FINDING MYSELF

I started to think, *maybe my dad being in my life wasn't meant
to be.*

I wasn't willing to accept the empty feeling inside for the
rest of my life, so I decided to go on a quest to find myself.

As I stepped onto this intentional path, entrepreneur-
ship fell into my lap. I was surrounded by people who were
thinking and dreaming BIG and naturally, I personally grew
because of all the incredible people in my environment. I was
moved and inspired. I was seeing the love and passion they
had to help others, and it was exactly what I knew I wanted
my life to be about.

I started asking myself, *why am I here, what am I meant to
do and what is my place in this big world?*

The path to my healing was unlocked.

As I leaned in and became open to the answers, I realized
that it was the unhappiness holding me back from feeling

good about myself, having a successful relationship with my family, or a partner. Through the lack of happiness, I could only view my life from the lens of a victim. In order to fill my own cup, I had to break the chain that kept me linked to the hurt and pain of my past. I felt called to make amends with everything and everyone that I felt had caused me pain. It wasn't about forgiving them for what they had done, but rather taking ownership for the role I played in how things turned out. I had to forgive myself; this is what it was *really* about. Forgiveness became my saving grace. It was the kind of forgiveness that released the weight I had been carrying on my shoulders for years. The kind that sets you free from everything you believed to be true and allows you to open your heart again.

My entire life shifted on July 5th, 2013, when my dad and I finally spoke. We went for a drive and exchanged the most truthful, raw, and honest words to each other. I'll admit, it was surprising. It's not something I longed for, but it's what I needed. I needed more than "this is my dad." I needed a deeper human connection to the person who helped bring me into this world. Feeling that connection was enough for me to put the past in the past.

When I recognized that we both longed for that connection, I felt ready and safe to share what was on my heart and even more ready, to let it all go. It was time to move forward and put the past behind us. The pain of my past consumed my world as I was stuck feeling sorry for myself and blaming my dad for everything that went wrong in my life. All the hurt and anger left my entire body and I finally had enough space to build a relationship with the most important person that I had forgotten about, myself.

I felt liberated from that one conversation with my dad and so I knew it was time to work through past relationships that I had unresolved feelings around. One conversation at a time, I felt myself feeling lighter and freer. A new version of myself had been born and as I continued to heal my childhood wounds, I fell in love with me.

All along, that was the missing piece.

This newfound relationship I established with myself opened my eyes to a whole new light. I found a love and confidence within that I had never experienced. I felt comfortable in my skin and open to whatever came my way. I stopped fixating on the illusion that someone else's love was supposed to complete me. Loving me, completed me.

It seemed I was last to find out about this big life changing secret, but it turns out I wasn't. Another break-up came and went, but this time I fought to harmonize the things that weren't right. I couldn't help but feel disappointed because it was my first time putting my all into a relationship. *I mustn't be cut out for this dating thing.*

The Universe had other plans for me because as it turns out, I had already met my soulmate when I was thirteen. Him and I had been best friends for years and I always used to tell him, "I'm just going to clone you," because I knew he would make the most perfect boyfriend and life partner. He was confident in himself and I admired how fiercely he loved and cared for the people in his life. He was selfless and enjoyed his life. These qualities were admirable and remarkable.

And there we were, both going through our own separate breakups. We decided to do what good friends do during heartache and transition—take a drive with no particular destination to sit in an empty parking lot, while drinking a half and half coffee with hot chocolate to talk about life.

There's a secret within this story that is significant that I've feared being judged for because it's caused me heavy guilt and shame. You see, he and I weren't like the scene from the movie, 13 Going on 30, where childhood best friends Jenna and Matty realize their bond was more than just friends; they fall in love, the end.

Our story was more complicated because while I was going through my own break-up, he was breaking up with one of my best friends.

As I share this, I can still feel that pit in my stomach all over again. *This isn't right, what will people think of me?* For a long time, I buried myself in the shame and guilt one would feel knowing they've developed feelings for their best friends ex. I knew the risk of following my heart.

Whenever we'd get asked, "how did you meet?" I felt my throat instantly tighten up, while the palms of my hands got sweaty. I would take a deep breath and give the most surface-level answer, "Oh you know, we've been friends for years! He went to the same high school as my sisters and his sister and I became best friends in high school. We've just been really great friends for years."

How was I going to live with the guilt?

The internal battle was something I had never felt before. I fought and cried about it with myself for many nights and so the next step revealed to follow my heart, and not succumb to pleasing others; this was radical self-love.

The Universe caught us off guard.

I never would have imagined us being in this position. As I struggled with what was happening, he continued to whisper in my ear, "follow your heart." It was almost a year into our relationship when I was finally able to let go of the guilt. A part of me had to realize that the chapter with my best friend wasn't meant to be open forever. On the other hand, I had to embrace that the Universe gave me exactly what I asked for; him. Not a duplicate or a clone. The universe gave me him.

Time stopped when we were together. We could sit for hours, talking about life and our dreams. We were at a place in our lives where we were certain about ourselves and had a bigger vision for where we were headed. We were both ready to find that person who felt independently complete within themselves. We were more than ready for any challenge that would help us become an even better version of who we already were.

YOU HOLD THE POWER

I spent a lot of time in my head wondering what people would think about me, us and the entire situation.

Would people understand my intentions? What would happen if it didn't work out?

What I knew for certain was that I couldn't fight against the love I felt and what my heart knew was meant to be in the moment. The bond and relationship we have is easy and I believe that's exactly what true love is. We should never feel like we have to work hard to be loved. For a long while, I thought nothing in life was easy and that getting what I wanted had to be a struggle because it's what I knew. But love, it's not something that needs to be forced.

Love begins and ends with you.

That is the ultimate piece to the puzzle, the treasure that we are all searching for. No one else's love is going to be the final ingredient that brings it all together. The love you have and give to yourself is what determines your self-worth. It determines what you say yes to, and what you say no to. It determines the relationships you have with others and the relationship you grow to have with yourself.

There comes a point when we must realize that self-sabotage hijacks incredible things from coming into our lives. That's exactly what my life had been about.

This chapter in my life isn't about a happily ever after because I found my soulmate. It's a happily ever after story because I found myself and decided to stop self-sabotaging.

There's a greek saying Gnothi Seauton, that translates to know thyself.

I came across it while reading A New Earth by Eckhart Tolle as I was on my healing journey, and it resonated with me. For many years I was walking through life, living unconsciously, running away and self-sabotaging my ability to love myself. I was just going through the motions with no real purpose or drive. The healing journey is what connected me within and changed my life.

It's easy for us to blame others for our disappointments, hold onto our pain and act as though we have no control over our lives. The reality is that *we hold the power*. From what we think, to what we speak out loud; it starts and ends with you. Initially it's uncomfortable because we're looking at ourselves from a bird's eye view, asking, "how can I do better?" and "what could I be doing differently?"

Believe it or not we are the creators of our reality, so be impeccable with your word. From the moment you wake up, to when you close your eyes to go to sleep, you get to choose what comes next. We have a choice to create our Heaven or to create our Hell. Which means, we get to be the authors of our story and have the power to change our narrative at any given moment. It begins with a choice. For a long time,

I didn't know I had a choice. I picked up a book called The Four Agreements by Don Miguel Ruiz and it's what saved me.

I took back control of my life, chapter by chapter. It helped me acknowledge the power I had in the words I spoke to myself and out loud to the Universe. With every word and thought, I was creating my own Hell. It was exhausting and didn't serve me. The same amount of energy I fueled into creating that reality could have been spent creating my Heaven. We always have a choice.

My choices were to forgive my dad and follow my heart. These decisions determined what could happen next.

The beauty is that we can always make new choices.

You don't have to chain the past to your ankles. It's easy for us to accept the stories we've grown up believing, but if the stories and the pain associated aren't serving you, let them go. They will get in the way of your happiness.

It's time to accept the gifts the universe is trying to bring you, so free your heart and lovingly embrace all that you are.

The Beauty in Feeling

DANA CLARK

AM I BROKEN?

Sometimes I feel as though I'm a flower sitting in the sun.

Grounded and planted, while letting the warm rays absorb into my skin to help me grow and heal into the woman I'm meant to be.

Nourishing me by giving me my vitamins, my warmth, and the comfort of feeling that, I too, deserve to be soaked up and seen by the world.

I was doing exactly that before I sat down to write.

Growing, in the sun. With sweat beaming on my forehead and sunscreen slightly leaking into my eyes, wondering why.

Why? I always ask myself.

Why am I so sensitive?

Why do I always seem to feel everything?

Why do I feel like I'm always the one who sits and thinks about everything?

Why do I feel alone in these feelings?

It feels like a burden to be constantly feeling all of the time.

Why do I feel like I am the only one who ever senses things?

Why do I feel like I hold onto things in my soul?

Why do I feel like I am the one who quietly thinks and feels things on the inside, while it seems like everyone else is feeling and thinking things on the outside?

I think to myself: *If I stop caring, I stop living.*

Feeling is a part of being alive. Sometimes feeling is painful, but it certainly reminds us that we are alive; humans in full form.

More questions, I ask.

Am I broken? Or is everyone else broken?

Am I the lucky one? Or are they the lucky ones?

The burden of feeling so deeply all of the time feels lonely, yet lucky. I've always lived in my head, and it's led me to sink deeply into who I am at my core. I've experienced my soul come out of my body, float above me, and speak directly to me.

This soul leads me. It guides me and best of all, it's made me into this feel-everything-all-at-once-no-matter-if-it's-warranted type of person.

A vessel, a soul in human form.

The most accurate way I can describe myself is someone who lives to be connected. To people, places, objects, ideas, the senses, and especially to humans.

This is my "socially acceptable" way of saying that *if my soul doesn't feel alive, and if I stop sensing and feeling things, I stop living.*

I don't mean living in the literal sense of life or death, but what I do mean is, living by being connected to yourself and others. The feeling of being awake; fully awake.

It sounds dramatic, I know, but that's how real it feels in my heart and head. It feels as though all my experiences and senses are all bundled up and given to me for a reason. To write, speak, think, and then *do* something about. So that I can show people that it's ok to *feel*, be sensitive, and feel lost in your heart, but still somehow understand your fiery passion to make change and do good in the world.

The first time I understood that I was different, was when I was eight-years-old. It was Christmas and I was sitting around my dinner table, joined by twenty-two of my closest relatives. A couple months prior, at Thanksgiving, someone had the idea of going around the table, one by one, and sharing with the group what we were most grateful for. I thought: *this is profound. Adults and kids of all ages, all openly talking about their feelings, and gratitude? What world am I living in? This is different but I like it.* I thought I'd bring back that fun and memorable moment I had of sharing and hearing *feelings at* Thanksgiving.

This idea was not supported. Some participated, most didn't, and even more looked at me like, *why is she bringing this up now? Can't we eat?* In my little eight-year-old mind, this is exactly how it played out. I felt stupid and alone, and like I was the only one out of these several family members who had the same basic need that I did: connection. This is one of the last times I asked to do this. I say *one* of the last times because I still bring up that memorable moment of exchanging gratitude amongst each other. I suggest it when

I'm feeling courageous enough to not take no's or eye rolling personally. Now I'm 26, and still feel like I'm fighting at most tables to create connections and make sensitivity, empathy, and feelings normalized.

I'm still trying to figure out why people don't like to share their emotions.

It feels inherent. My basic need is to feel, to outwardly show my insides. Why not for others? What happened to them? What made them turn inwards?

When someone is rude or unpleasant, I can't help but wonder if they're going through something. I immediately respond to the person with compassion. Firstly, I self reflect and secondly I offer empathy, as I don't know their situation. This person may have shown someone who they truly are and someone might have made them feel shame for this vulnerability.

If so, this person is now walking around, thinking their internal desires don't matter, or they need fixing. In my opinion, this is our problem as a society. We are so busy trying to fix ourselves and others, that we end up missing out on people's beautiful souls, hearts *and* feelings.

IS THIS A GIFT?

For a very long time, this sense of feeling overly "connected" or "sensitive" felt like a curse. I felt as though I was chosen to be the one who carries the feelings of others on their shoulders. Tired, distracted, and overworked because instead of being present, it feels like I'm analyzing and attacking all of the world's disconnect, discontent and heartbreak all at once.

Wouldn't it be easier and less complicated if I could just turn it off?

I think back to my eight-year-old self and I now understand that the only thing I wanted was to bring people together. That dinner table was my peace offering. It was my plea to bring people together emotionally, by mending our disconnects. I wanted to show people that so many of our worldly problems can be solved simply by listening, loving, and understanding our fellow humans. My eight-year-old self didn't know that this is what I'd eventually build two companies on. With authentic human-to-human connection.

I took this sensitive trait of mine and thought, *there must be others out there who feel like this too—others who feel more like themselves when they've fully exposed their inner most human form.*

I was right.

I started Heroic Humans in 2017 with the intention to inspire, celebrate and empower all people from different walks of life. This intention grew much bigger than I anticipated. It grew to become a movement that features acts of heroism and real stories from real people across the world. It's a space for people to feel seen and heard for exactly who they are and what they've been through using our podcast, blog, events, and community involvement.

The reason I know I'm not alone anymore is because I've had the honour of interviewing people from all across this beautiful world who are sensitive souls. These souls end up creating beautiful, impactful, and long-lasting inspired change for the people around them. They too, feel called to make a difference and bring people together.

The most profound thing I've learned is that we all feel. No matter what the cause or detriment is, we're all impacted by the deepest crevasses of our hearts and bodies. Although we're all in different parts of the world, with different experiences, privileges and circumstances, we all experience somewhat of the same emotions. Joy, excitement, and love, as well as trauma, guilt, shame, fear, grief, and heartbreak are more universal than we think. If we begin to talk about and understand human experiences then we can relate with *feeling.* We are that much closer to bridging the gap against the systems, ideologies, fears, and communities that are keeping us apart.

There was one common theme that I noticed through the conversations I had with these brave people. The theme of connection was always present. We all want connection in some way or another. We crave it, seek it and demand it. We create it, pray for it and write about it. We even watch it on screen and read about it in books.

Connection has, in one way or another touched all of our lives. Whether it's connection with ourselves during our healing, personal growth, self-love and acceptance, or connection with our partners, family, friends, co-workers and acquaintances. Whether it's connection to a place or destination or connection to our highest purpose—we all know that we need it.

This sparked another question in me, *how can I make connection "cool"?* So, I reflected on how I could create more of this in our day-to-day lives.

I launched *Cool To Connect* in May 2020. *Cool To Connect* is a simple, yet effective tool where people get to feel connected to others, and themselves through the art of conversation and active listening.

Cool To Connect is set out to change the way we look at connection. It would've been the perfect tool to pass around that dinner table all those years ago. Frankly, most people need a prompt or reason to connect and these cards provide exactly that; mission accomplished.

I'M NOT BROKEN, AND NEITHER ARE YOU.

If someone would've told me that my sense of connection and need to feel was simply a gift, and not a soul-sucking curse, it could've saved me a lot of confusion. I will admit that I wouldn't change this path I've been given because finding my way out of confusion was an opportunity to create something the world needed.

A piece of my purpose is to affirm you that you are not broken. You're not put on this planet to have someone, or something alter and change you. You're good enough as you are, and that *thing* you've been thinking of this entire time is worthy of being seen, celebrated and acknowledged.

I know that *feeling* can be painfully uncomfortable. I feel like it's a responsibility to *feel*. Like it's heavy, unwarranted, and comes when you least expect it. It comes in all forms. In joyful, beautiful, and sometimes even hurtful ways.

I wouldn't say that my fear to feel is gone; absolutely not. What I do know about being a feeler is that we're the lucky ones, and when I'm on the brink of a big feeling or big sense of self, I'm onto something. Something special that I hope will end up connecting and bringing more people together.

It's up to us, together, to keep talking about the ways in which we feel. Your feelings are worthy and they matter. They are profound, existential, and completely, and beautifully yours.

Own that. You're one of the chosen ones, the feelers, who's here to teach the series of lessons you've acquired.

Now sit back beautiful flower, and feel the sun on your pores as it leaks into your soul and nourishes your heart. Feel your warm tender heart begin to feed your beautiful being.

Sink into yourself.

Grow, laugh, heal, breathe.
And know that you are whole.

Destined To Be This Way

JOVANA BOROJEVIC

"You're going to die before you're thirty."

That's what my doctor kept telling me as I told her not to weigh me again this visit. This wasn't the first time I was here, and I knew it wouldn't be the last. I would once again sit in her cold, bare office and look at her dead in the eyes while she told me I was suffering from a severe case of Polycystic Ovarian Syndrome and that my fatty liver disease was really worsening. I'd leave again, numb, and I'd go home. Her words didn't touch me, they never even came close.

I was twenty-five years old, and at that point in my life I could not walk up the stairs without running out of breath, I could not tie my own shoes, and sometimes it hurt to breathe; but this was my normal, and I never questioned it. I truly believed that I was destined to be "this way," and so I had given up on a body that seemed determined to fail me anyways.

Every day, my mind would invite me to sit and eat until it hurt to breathe just to fill the void that came with a body that I just wished I could fix so desperately. Every day was full of empty promises about how I would love myself one day if only I could get all the nasty fat to melt away. And every day ended the same—still waiting for that special Monday, waiting for another opportunity to hopefully decide that I was something worth fighting for, that I was something worth loving, knowing deep down that I would give up on myself again anyways.

I avoided mirrors like the plague because I could not stand to look at the failure that would be there looking back at me. I would catch glimpses of my horrifying body as I walked by, but those moments never lasted more than a few seconds. A few seconds of looking is all it took for my mind to scream *YOU'RE DISGUSTING, you'll never be enough, I hate you.*

How could I be enough for anybody, for anything, looking the way I did? If anything I was too much; too much fat, too much gross, too much cellulite, too much jiggle, too much stomach, too much thighs...too much. For me, shrinking all my *too much* into *just enough* felt entirely impossible.

I was surely destined to be trapped in this life-long burden of hating myself, this burden of not being enough. It seemed that each time I caught that glimpse in the mirror, all I could see was how far away I was from that state of enoughness, all I could see were all the pieces of me that were wrong. Each time I looked, the burden of simply existing felt heavier and the concept of feeling enough felt so far off in the distance.

—

It was a cold night in January of 2016, and as I was finishing my second bag of Cheetos for the evening, I remember feeling the pressure become heavy on my stomach, and my daily mental-torture-soundtrack quietly began.

How could you do this again? Why can't you just fucking stop? You're still beyond disgusting.

This was the inner dialogue I was used to, the soundtrack of my mind. The familiar words pulsed through my brain as I stared at the ceiling in a monotone state of numbness. It had been many years of the same repeated daily cycle, that I already knew how to tune out and ignore it—how to silence my noise. Instead, I reached for the cookies, throwing my mind into cruise control and pushing the shame away; *it's okay, I'll try again next Monday.*

The next morning felt like an uncomfortable blur, as it usually did, but one decision felt extremely clear. For some reason, I had decided I was going to step on the scale that day. I hadn't weighed myself in over two years, because truthfully I was scared. *That* number was controlling me. *That* number was ruling what I was allowed to do and what I wasn't, who I was allowed to be and who I wasn't, and most importantly how happy I was allowed to be. For years my solution to *that* number was avoidance because if you don't see it, it can't control you, right?

I slowly walked towards my bathroom, almost tip-toeing in hopes that my mind wouldn't hear me, in hopes that it wouldn't make *fun* of the number I would see. I stepped inside clenching my fists, staring down at my dusty scale that sat underneath the sink. I could feel my heart beat faster and faster, throbbing throughout my body, pulsating softly at my fingertips. The last time I remembered being here I weighed in at 250 pounds of disappointment, and that was already really high, so how bad could this be?

I stepped up, inhaled, and looked down...

305 pounds. *305 pounds?* Three hundred, and five pounds!

That's *the* number that finally terrified me. There was something about seeing that three I never thought I would see, that caused me to spiral into what felt like the deepest depths of anxiety; like a fire being automatically sparked inside of me. I stood there, still, looking down at my disgusting body, and waves of paralyzing shame just kept washing over me.

I don't know what happened and I can't really explain, but within those few seconds something stronger than me took over my brain, and the words **no this can't be me** bounced back and forth within the walls of my dizzy skull, as all of what little sensation was left in my body seemed to melt away. *How could I have done this to myself?* I had asked this question before, but this time it felt different. This time as the waves of disgust subsided I felt fear, true genuine fear.

You're going to die before you're thirty, echoed throughout my brain and I could feel each of my doctor's words as they traveled down my spine, punching between each vertebra on their journey to my gut.

I'm going to die before I'm thirty.

This was it. I somehow knew that it was now or never that I was going to take back control of my life, and deep down in my soul, I knew that for me this meant I was going to have to save myself—but I had no idea what that would **actually** mean.

From that day forward I decided I was done being a prisoner to my own body—but little did I know that my physical body was going to be the **least** of my worries.

DESTINATION: "LOVE"

Over the next year, I changed my life drastically. I stopped eating certain foods cold turkey, and going to the gym every day became my new reality. There were moments when I stopped in awe of myself, in awe of how I was able to make such a powerful change in a way that I could only describe at the time as, effortlessly. It was like I was on a new type of cruise control, riding down the happiness highway towards *Destination: Love!*

As I stepped on the scale each and every single day, I felt relieved and motivated to continue down this path I had set out for myself; the path to discovering a version of me that was no longer shameful and disgusting.

This was the first time in my life I felt truly accomplished, truly proud, like I was finally doing everything right, and as my outer layers started melting away, I finally felt like I had a reason to stay. I felt like I was in full control; in the driver's seat of my life; and neither food nor *that* number could control me any longer.

—

For the first time in my life, I finally did it, and I was so proud of myself. In just over one year I had lost 140 pounds! I reversed my fatty liver disease and took control of my health. I was well on my way to living beyond thirty! That's really where this story should end, where I thought it would end; because I finally stopped waiting for next Monday and I reached my life's biggest goal and purpose. I was finally thin, and I was thriving. I looked and felt amazing, and I could fit into whatever I wanted. *That* number was finally something I wasn't ashamed of, I was actually proud of it and wanted to scream it from the rooftops. *This was it, right? When we finally get here that's when we're allowed to love ourselves because we finally have a loveable, beautiful body, right?*

So, why did I hate myself? I remember sitting, deep in confusion. It felt like I had finally made it down the love highway to the *love yourself* train station, and I was waiting for the train to arrive, but each time it passed by my body felt too frozen to hop on. I didn't understand—why did I feel such a strong sense of hate for myself in this "ideal" body, more than when I was wearing *my idea* of disgusting?

I walked past my mirror, naked, wanting to admire myself, but as I stood there the familiar waves of shame came crash-ing against the shores of my soul harder than they ever had and I suddenly felt like I was drowning. Standing still, once again looking down at my disgusting body, in utter disbelief of how I could still be feeling this way.

But this time, I thought, I *know how to fix this feeling, I know what makes me feel good. That* number just needed to come down once again. I stepped off the scale, and as my feet met the ground, I felt a pull of heaviness that I had never experienced before. I was ashamed to admit that I felt like I was once again failing myself.

—

I became addicted to losing weight because I thought this was the key to accepting myself. I was addicted to the way it felt, and the rush of happiness it gave me—even if it was temporary. I craved it, I wanted more and I got more.

Weighing myself daily quickly turned into three times a day, and I felt like I was slowly losing my mind because I couldn't understand how each evening I was 0.8 pounds heavier than the morning when I had done everything right. My life became a forever revolving door of *never enoughness* because as soon as I would lose the next five pounds, the five I never thought about came right after. It was just never enough, **I was just never enough.**

I would stand in front of the mirror for a few seconds a day, searching for new ways to mold into a woman worthy of her own love, ignoring that my eyes had sunk into their fragile sockets. All I could see was the loose skin around my belly that made itself seemingly too comfortable in places where my fat used to be. Stretch marks covering inches upon inches of my skin, and again I was reminded of how much of a failure my body was and of how much fixing was left to do.

It wasn't something I could grasp at the time, but I was headed towards the other end of a very dangerous spectrum, never giving myself the time and grace to sit comfortably right where I was, right where my body needed me.

I spewed words of hate towards myself every time I felt natural hunger and I punished myself every time I ate six asparagus spears instead of five, and somewhere deep in the depths of my mind I could hear a distant voice asking—"Is this what it really means to be healthy and alive?" I couldn't see that the same food that was controlling my life before, *that* same number, was doing the exact same thing as it always had; I just wasn't looking, I wasn't truly listening. I just couldn't see myself.

I was slowly trading physical ailments for mental ones and it started feeling like I was pawning off pieces of my soul at the cost of another pound down, leaving me drained and angry with myself and anybody who couldn't understand why I needed to keep going.

It became difficult to avoid myself as I always had, and I spent days locked in the grooves of my own mind, flowing down the canals of hate that I had dug out and filled over the years. I spent days wondering, just wondering how to make it end. I spent days avoiding those I loved most, stuck in a room with just my own thoughts, doing my best to tune them out as they floated closer and closer to the forefront of my consciousness.

I hated being with others but I hated being alone, and day after day I felt like I was losing touch with myself and any sense of feeling at peace, at home. The hiding spots within the depths of my mind, where I stowed the truths I had been trying to ignore, became overcrowded. I constantly tried to switch off all of my brain's light switches, once again only hoping that if I never had to see the mess I created, it wouldn't really be there.

But that's not how it works, and the longer I tried to avoid that which I was being called to see and acknowledge, the bigger and more aggressively it showed up in my consciousness when I least expected it.

—

I was preparing to take a shower one random Wednesday, and as I walked past the same full-length mirror I've had for years, I caught a glimpse as I usually did. My initial *you're disgusting* instinct took over, but as I went to place one foot in front of the other, something didn't allow me to walk away, something invited me to actually stay. At this moment I couldn't hear my thoughts, not the ones I usually did. The silence felt daunting and unnatural; not real. Was it okay that I didn't know how to react? Was it okay that something felt different?

"So this is me, huh?" were the next words I heard. I could remember all of the days past that I had looked at myself here, but I couldn't remember the last time I had seen myself, I mean really *seen myself*, and as I felt my own gaze pierce through my soul, I was suddenly looking into the depths of my own sadness.

It was at this moment that I remembered the words of a friend of mine who had once told me; "Jovana, I know it feels like you're not doing enough, but I promise you, you are. Tonight when you go home, look yourself in the eyes and just say *I love you.*" I remember scoffing at the notion, at how laughable and pointless it would be to do something so meaningless, so simple—so I never did. But at this moment, the universe gifted me her words, and invited me to lean into silence and simply try.

So, I tried to do what I thought was the simplest thing a human can do—look in the mirror and say "I love you." My heartbeat increased, and I felt the familiar soft thuds landing in the tips of my fingers. I thought I was going crazy, but as I made eye contact with myself, I felt an energetic shift, and I leaned in, to break the silence out loud:

"I I..."

"I lov..."

"I...."

I couldn't do it, no words came; warm tears just rolled down my face and the familiar thoughts came crashing.

How could you love something so nasty?

In that space between the silence and the oh-so-familiar was where I found grief, sadness, and loss. It was in that space that I had turned the light switches in my mind on, even for a moment, and saw all that I had been neglecting. At that moment I realized that *that* number wasn't worth anything in this world if I couldn't *see* the reflection in the mirror; if I couldn't recognize that girl.

I truly felt the weight of realizing that for so long I had been searching for happiness on the outside because I thought that's where it lived; because I was too afraid of what I might find within. It was clear that I had no idea who I was—beyond the weight, the body, *the* number—who was Jovana? The question reverberated through me and I felt a little dizzy, the hairs on the back of my neck standing.

I had spent all these years as a *human becoming* that I forgot to be a *human being*, and in the process of constantly doing, I lost sight of the fact that I had been dropping pieces of my soul as I ran towards what I thought was the answer to all my problems. For years I had failed to acknowledge my entire existence as more than pounds of flesh. All those years spent ignoring *that* number, and then fixating on it, were years all spent distracting myself from who I was really meant to be.

I knew that it was time to finally meet myself; face to soul. That night I promised to show up for myself every single day, regardless of what happened the day before. I promised to acknowledge the pain I had been hiding from, no matter how hard it was, and to practice expressing love to my human until the words turned into feelings that lit my soul on fire.

I spent day after day in front of my mirror, uttering the words "I love you. You are strong. You are enough. You are WORTHY." Day after day, failed attempt after failed attempt.

I apologized to my body for all the years I spent screaming at it and classifying it into groups of "good enough" and "needs improvement." I held it and I said:

"Thank you for giving my mind a home, no matter how harmful it has been to you. Thank you for keeping my heartbeat flowing through me and continuously moving my feet."

I slowly started to feel my soul's embrace and I was finally *seeing* myself, without expectations of what I was "supposed" to *look* like.

I heard my voice get louder with each extra second I stayed. I stopped questioning how I could feel fierce but gentle, strong but weak, so sure and so confused at the same time; because I realized not all Q's needed A's. I accepted that it was ok that I knew nothing and everything at the same time. I finally realized that the very mind I was afraid to face daily was where my success lied—I couldn't run from all the overcrowded hiding places anymore, their contents had spilled out right in front of me.

For the first time in my life, I allowed myself to make the decision that I was something worth loving, and for the first time in my life, I truly felt the truth of knowing that the way

I looked, and that *that* number, had absolutely nothing to do with it.

DESTINATION: HOME

It was never just about my body or the weight I wanted to lose, it was so much more. It was about the reality that I had created in which I believed strongly that I was never enough, so therefore, I was never going to be. I wanted to lose the shame, the guilt, and the sadness that I had been suppressing for years. I wanted to avoid the uncomfortable and hide the negative so that I would never have to face unwanted feelings.

I wanted so badly to see myself, to feel love for ME; the same home where my sister, mother, and father came for love and security. I wanted to stop ignoring the thoughts that ran through my brain—but I couldn't pick and choose, I had to feel it ALL. In order to soothe the pain that lived in my heart and help it fade away, I had to give the negative thoughts the time of day. It was on me to open my eyes and lean in.

I thought that changing my outer appearance would somehow fix me, somehow help me feel that I was enough, despite all the brokenness, but changing outwardly never changed my inner landscape. No matter how much I altered the outside, and no matter how much I did or did not eat, the person living within was always *always* **always** going to be...me.

And that was something so much more than skin deep, that I failed to see. I had no idea that my body had nothing to do with my enoughness. It was merely the vessel that carried the mind that housed the thoughts I chose to believe—and I held the power to change them.

Behind my daily mental-torture-soundtrack lie cries for attention in the only way my mind knew how to get it. It was my soul's attempt to tell me that I couldn't mold myself to be something that would finally be enough; **because I already was, and always would be**, I just needed to believe it.

The cure to feeling *not enough* did not lie on the surface of my skin. It pulsated softly underneath, between the depths of my human, waiting for me to feel it's humming rhythm finally reaching deep within.

I reclaimed my mind, body, soul, and life when I **decided** that I was deserving in my entirety at any moment. Yes, it was a decision. Not an easy one, but one that was necessary. You see, I did things that I thought would fix me because I thought love was the destination, but you see, love is the *journey*.

In order to live a life in which I was able to first accept, and then love myself entirely, I had to come face to face with, and erase, the illusion that I would ever find happiness by swimming in the shallow ends of my physicality; never choosing to dive in deep, never choosing to come home.

You are not broken, you are always whole.
You are not perfect, but you are always enough.

Destination: Home.

about the authors

ASHLEY-ANN PEREIRA AND TINA ADDORISIO

Ashley-Ann and Tina, founders of The Collective Voice Project were inspired to bring this group together after experiencing their own transformation while in the process of becoming authors. Ashley-Ann is the author of *The Key to Happiness*. She believes everyone's story matters and shares her message on stages along with coaching coaches on how to impact their community by writing books. Tina is the author of Amazon's best-selling book called *Beautiful Becoming*. She helps bloggers and writers organize and self-publish their content into books that allow them to stand out in their industries. Ashley-Ann and Tina are inspired by stories and believe that writing a book is about who you become along the way. They continue to explore ways to support individuals who want to share their stories.

Ashley-Ann and Tina would like to acknowledge all the incredible authors that committed to sharing their stories from the heart. The process of authentic and transparent expression has its challenges and they honour the women for connecting to their true north of serving our readers.

@thestudiopress | @ashleyann.me | @tina_addorisio

MARGARITA KALIKA

Margarita Kalika is an earthy storyteller and poet capturing the wild beauty and magic in all things. She is co-creator of Wild Luna Paper Co., a creative shop of paintings and poetry to uplift and ground the spirit. As a writer, book lover, and tarot reader, Margarita uses the ancient craft of storytelling to inspire and guide seekers to walk their true path.

Margarita is grateful to her four wild sisters for their heaping spoonfuls of love, and to her mama and papa for building a home on new ground and telling the old Russian tales. This chapter is dedicated to them, to my fellow soul sisters in this collection, to you wise reader, and to the trees gifting papered land for words to walk on.

@thelunafairy | www.thelunanook.com | @wildlunapaperco

MELISSA SEGUIN

Melissa Seguin is a self-described hope dealer. With more than 20 years in the field of health and wellness, Melissa empowers women and families to live life on purpose and with passion.

Melissa loves all things nature and being outdoors! She continues to lead an active life beyond 40 and rightly so as she has an active partner and two active boys to keep up with and teach them to show up every day as their most authentic and connected selves.

To the little boy with big brown eyes, the beautiful soul who knew he needed to come in and who knew I was ready. You made me a mama. Thank you for trusting me to be a part of your journey and for teaching me daily what unconditional love looks like.

To the second little boy, spunky and sweet, who gifted me with a beautiful home birth. Your knowing that I had healed enough to birth you at home is something I will always be grateful for, even if you did come on the only day I told you not to.

To my hubs, always ready to roll with the pivots in this life. Your support and partnership is one of my greatest joys. Your trust in me amazes me and I'm grateful our children chose you as their papa.

To Lidia, your energy healing was the catalyst for my family's destiny. I never imagined that motherhood would come to me in one of the most relaxing hours of my life on your table.

To my own courageous soul, for digging in and pushing past all the mind chatter. A reminder that the healing continues to happen when space is provided. Thank you for trusting yourself.

@melissaseguin11

ASHLEY ANTONIETTA

Ashley Antonietta is a sucker for love. Her life experiences around relationships and self-discovery have made her believe in and realign with the women she is today. She continues to spread love and wisdom to those around her as they seek it, in hopes to empower people on all walks of life. When you go inward, and discover the type of love you seek from those around you, the law of attraction will always prevail. She believes in designing a life from within consciously and purposely.

Thank you to the men who came into my life. For you mirrored parts of myself I needed to shed and parts of myself I needed to love harder.

To my family, thank you for your support and love always.

To my husband, thank you for your love, your warmth and your tenderness.

To my baby, as I patiently await your arrival, thank you for amplifying my life, my strength and my commitment to myself so that I can continue to live life consciously and openly. I love you.

ashleyantonietta@gmail.com | @ashleyantonietta

SHANNON HARLOW

Shannon Harlow embraces her most treasured job as a wife and mother with unwavering devotion. She loves spending time at the cottage, walking her dogs in nature and participating in local yoga classes. A person devoted to peace, love, and compassion for all living beings; Shannon enjoys a plant-based lifestyle and became a culinary nutritionist to share her love of vegetarian cooking with others.

I would like to acknowledge my kids; Sara, Trent, Sydney, and my husband for their strength, courage, and faith. I'm thankful for their unwavering devotion to our family, especially Syd as she was in the accident with me and has travelled this long road to healing with me.

DEVLYN SARAH

Devlyn is a mental health advocate who has personally experienced the struggles of mental illnesses. She has worked and volunteered in the health care field for many years. Her goal is to spread awareness and show anyone struggling that it is possible to lead a contented life with disorders and after trauma.

Dedicated to all those who went on my journey with me, to my father who showed me strength was not solely external and to my mother who never gave up on me even when I gave up on myself.

DANIELLE ROSA

Danielle is a self-empowerment facilitator helping others find, understand and utilize the natural resources within themselves to create a life of health, wealth and happiness. From Interior Design, Feng Shui, Life and Business Coaching, Danielle has come to understand the creation process of consciously designing a life you love.

I would like to thank all the people, experiences, growth, and journey of my life experience that has brought me to where I am today. Because without them, I wouldn't be the person I have come to be.

To my mom, dad and best friend, Jackie; thank you for all the love you brought to my life and for still being a part of my journey till this day. I feel you with me every day. Thank you for being a helping hand in directing me to my Inner Knowing and what true, divine love is. I hope we have made a positive difference in someone's journey by sharing our story. I love you eternally.

Danielle_rosa@me.com | @Daniellerosa11

@divine_design_living | divinedesignliving.onuniverse.com

DANA CLARK

Dana Clark is a host, entrepreneur, and advocate. She is the founder and creator of Heroic Humans, a global social impact movement, and Cool To Connect, an initiative that creates connection tools and resources. Dana is the recipient of the Notable Life's Mindful Millennial Award, and strives to make human experiences more relatable, conversational, and impactful.

To those on my journey who have always encouraged me to create a beautiful life and strive for all of my crazy ideas and pursuits;

I wouldn't be me without you. My chapter is dedicated to my mom, Susan Elliott, the most hardworking and brave woman I know, who shows me daily that you truly can "have it all."

@danasusanclark

@cooltoconnect | cooltoconnect.com

@theheroichumans | heroichumans.com

JOVANA BOROJEVIC

Jovana is a self-neutrality and self-love advocate whose mission is to work with women around the world in guiding them back to their truest form of self. She spent years struggling with and defining her worth by her weight until she plunged into her most untapped place; her soul. She hopes her story about coming back home to meet herself and discover her true worth will give women the courage to hold their own hand and step into their brightest light.

To Una; thank you for being my infinite butterfly. To mama and tata; thank you for shining light on all the places I couldn't see by myself.

@jovanafit | @xjbeepoetry